ZEBO
Liquid

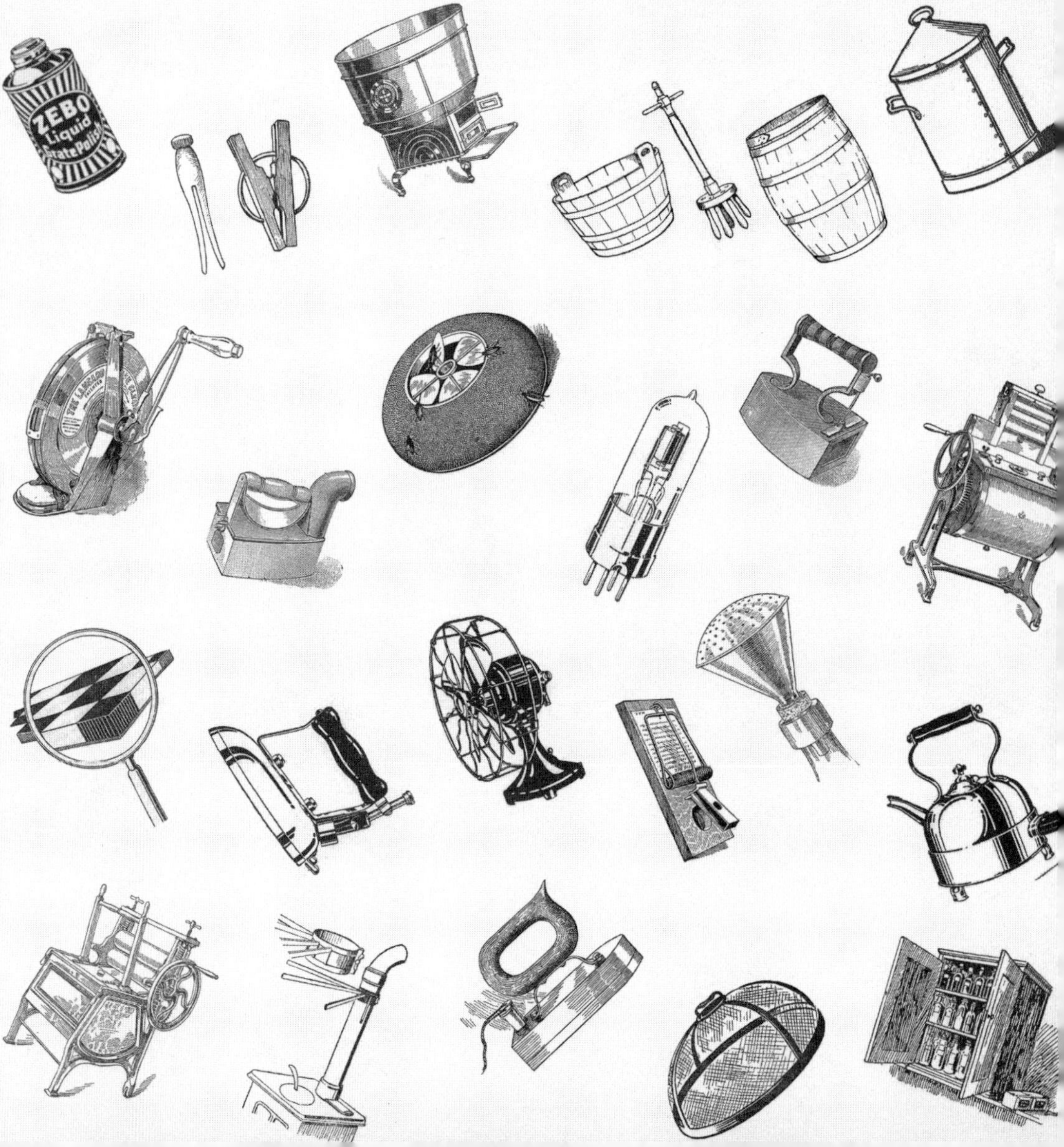
ZEBO
Liquid
Grate Polish

ELBOW GREASE

ELBOW GREASE

HOW OUR GRANDMOTHERS AND GREAT-GRANDMOTHERS KEPT HOUSE

JACQUELINE PERCIVAL

CHAPLIN BOOKS

First published in 2011 by Chaplin Books

Copyright © Jacqueline Percival

ISBN 978-0-9565595-3-1

All rights reserved. No part of this publication may be reproduced, stored in any retrieval system or transmitted in any form or by any means, electronic, mechanical, photocopying, recording or otherwise, without the prior written permission of the copyright holder for which application should be addressed in the first instance to the publishers. No liability shall be attached to the author, the copyright holder or the publishers for loss or damage of any nature suffered as a result of reliance on the reproduction of any of the contents of this publication or any errors or omissions in its contents.

A CIP catalogue record for this book is available from The British Library.

Design by Helen Taylor

Printed in the UK by Ashford Colour Press

Chaplin Books
1 Eliza Place
Gosport PO12 4UN
Tel: 023 9252 9020
www.chaplinbooks.co.uk

Thanks to Amanda Field, Linda Hall, Robert Smith,
Tina Toms-Pearce, Penny Ward, Andy Wing,
my parents for bringing me up to appreciate work
and research properly done, Spot and Mike,
and everyone at Gosport Discovery Centre.

CONTENTS

Introduction 1

Chapter One: Clean it (housework) 7

Chapter Two: Wash it (laundry work) 61

Chapter Three: Kill it (pests in the home) .. 119

Conclusion 137

Glossary 140

Bibliography 141

Index 144

INTRODUCTION

It's 2am. A strange noise coming from your kitchen makes you sit bolt upright in bed. Is it a burglar? A visiting cat? You light a candle and tiptoe downstairs, avoiding the places where the stair-treads creak. Arming yourself with a sturdy old shoe that you keep on the bottom step for just such an occasion, you advance to the kitchen door and silently open it. Inside, you discover hundreds of cockroaches swarming over the floor and partying in the darkness. Systematically you lay about them with the shoe, reducing as many as you can to pulp before sweeping up the corpses and sending their relations back from whence they came with a satisfying sweep of your candle. Finally you shut the door and return to bed, uncomfortably aware that tomorrow night you'll almost certainly be doing this all over again.

It had been a long, hard day: you'd scrubbed the kitchen table with sand and skinned your knuckles; you'd spent precious seconds picking squashed bits of cauliflower out of a strainer; you'd dropped a shirt into a puddle as you were pegging it onto the line and had to wash it again by hand; the apple pie had burned because you'd guessed at the temperature rather than putting in the piece of paper that told you how hot the oven was; and to cap it all, you'd had a couple of minutes to check the butcher's bill and discovered that you'd been charged for meat you hadn't ordered. All in all you were pretty relieved to get to bed, and none too pleased to have to get up in the middle of the night to beat cockroaches to death.

Most modern householders would be more than mildly perturbed at the thought of an army of cockroaches making merry in the kitchen, and probably few would think of scrubbing their tables with sand, but anyone running a home before World War II would have done a lot of things that we no longer do, and that is the subject of this book.

Housekeeping and homemaking were dangerous occupations in the nineteenth and early twentieth centuries, and wash-day was almost certainly the most hazardous.

Commonly used chemicals were toxic or caustic, washing-soda could burn holes in cloth (and therefore skin), and some early washing machines featured an exposed electric motor clamped to the base. Housewives learned to treat the tools of their trade with care and respect, and relied on the advice and information in popular housekeeping manuals. Although 'Mrs Beeton' is probably the best known – her *Book of Household Management* was first published in 1861 and reprinted many times afterwards – there were scores of similar books available, each with its own target audience. Some catered for small incomes, some for the wealthy, some for women with servants, some for women without, and some were written specifically for women keeping house in India at the time of the Raj.

There were books with illustrations and books with densely packed text, small paper-covered pamphlets and huge multi-volume encyclopaedia with coloured plates and lavish detail. Some have been read almost to extinction, their pages scuffed and loose, the bindings worn and stained; others look as if they have never been opened. They were written by journalists, soap manufacturers, sanitary officials, newspapers, and a wide variety of 'experts' on everything from laundry work and plain cookery to home nursing and childbirth. Many of the titles published in the 1930s – a boom-time for advice books – hinted at the joys of domesticity, as in Helen Simpson's *The Happy Home*, or the satisfaction of organisation, as in Garth and Wrench's *Home Management*. Despite (or maybe because of) the undeniable cosy charm of such titles, many middle-class couples elected to move away from their family bases so they could rear their children without unwelcome input from their own parents. This inevitably dislocated the mother-daughter bond that had for generations handed down the family's folkways and wisdom, and the young wife either had to learn

1   Hammerton p.610.

housekeeping and child-rearing the hard way, or turn to a competent source such as an advice manual. Some of the advice offered may seem both archaic and unreal today, but it is worth remembering that with few labour-saving devices, women spent many more hours cleaning and cooking than they do now. We may think that because our cupboards are stuffed with a plethora of cleaning products to tackle everything from bathroom taps to laminate floors, and because there are even programmes about cleaning on prime-time TV, that our homes are worthy of the most exacting lifestyle magazine. The perhaps surprising truth is that housekeeping standards were far higher in the nineteenth and early twentieth centuries than they are today.

Marriage and domesticity were idealised as the pinnacle of achievement for women – 'it does not matter what a girl is going to be or do in after life', said the editor of the two-volume *Concise Household Encyclopaedia* in the late 1930s, 'she is handicapped unless she really knows how to keep house'.[1] Other 1930s books referred to what has been called the 'cult of home' in glowing, almost spiritual terms: home was seen as 'a shrine of married love, a haven of rest for hubby…a retreat…a refuge in time of trouble'.[2] The reality, however, was that many women embarked on a life of unremitting slog and toil when they married. Most of their efforts would have been concentrated on basic everyday cleaning and laundry work and, if they were unlucky enough to have cockroaches, lice, fleas or any other pests resident on the premises, or indeed on their bodies, they would have spent much time and energy trying to get rid of them. Home may well have been a haven of rest for 'hubby' and a refuge for the family, but at a time when every surface had to be scoured or scrubbed, it was a lot of work to keep it that way.

2 *Every Woman's Book of Home-Making* p.3.

I was extremely lucky in my own female examples of domesticity, having been taught by my mother to do things 'properly' around the house (even though I rarely do) and having had grandmothers who kept their homes spick and span with few labour-saving appliances and a lot of elbow-grease. One grandmother made dandelion wine, whitened her front step with donkeystone and did her washing in a copper, and the other polished her leather sofa with milk, made wonderful blackcurrant jam and kept a beautiful flower garden. Having slummed around in bedsits and shared houses for some years doing no housework whatsoever, I was intrigued to discover after I got married and had to start doing some, that housekeeping manuals were not only easily available in junk shops but were actually quite useful. Anyone nowadays who wants to reconstruct a housewife's day, or know what old washing machines looked like, or what the servants did all day, will probably find all the information they need in an old housekeeping manual – and they can also count their lucky stars that they no longer have to pick cauliflower out of the sieve or squash cockroaches with old shoes.

CHAPTER ONE

CLEAN IT...

...Housework

The average twenty-first century house can be cleaned from top to bottom without too much physical effort: surfaces can be wiped clean in seconds, vacuum-cleaners are light-weight (there are even robot vacuum-cleaners that will do the vacuuming for you) and modern thinking sees no virtue in pointless work. Even the need for spring-cleaning, that old-fashioned trial of strength, has been eliminated. It has not always been this easy. This chapter describes the ways our grandmothers and great-grandmothers cleaned, scrubbed and polished their homes, the products and equipment they used to do it, and the risks they ran.

A SNOW-WHITE STEP

One of the iconic images of housework is that of a woman on her hands and knees cleaning the front doorstep and the semi-circular area of pavement bounded by the swing of her arm from right to left. Step cleaning was part of the morning's routine work in many parts of the UK until well into the 1960s, and was done partly as an expression of self-proclaimed virtue and partly because many women apparently found great satisfaction in the sight of a freshly cleaned snow-white step, especially in a dingy, smoke-grimed neighbourhood.

There are stories of housewives getting up early to be the first one out to clean the step or the first to get the washing on the line and pick up the early gossip; women in close-knit working-class communities did their social networking over the garden wall, in the local shop or in the street, swapping stories and did-you-ever's as they went about their day's work.

There was a particular way to clean a front step, as with so many domestic tasks, and girls received instruction from their mothers in 'the right way'. First it was swept to remove dust, then it was washed – top, front and sides – with water and a flannel. After wetting it again, it was rubbed from side to side with hearthstone, sometimes known as donkeystone, making a hollow scratchy sound like bricks rubbing together. Hearthstone was cheap: in the 1890s three pieces could be bought for a penny from oil-shops, which sold paint, turpentine and various household sundries such as lamp oil. To finish off the job, the flannel was used again to prevent the chalky-white coating from drying in streaks or patches.

TAKE A POUND OF PIPEMAKERS' CLAY....

Open the average cleaning cupboard today and you'll find a host of branded products that can eliminate stains, dirt and fingermarks in seconds. You may have bought the product because you saw a TV commercial for it, or a big display in the supermarket. In the relatively recent past the range of products was more limited, but the variety of surfaces to be cleaned – everything from brass taps to stone steps – meant that while some products were available in the shops, others could be made at home from the raw ingredients. Here's a list from the 1930s of basic cleaning products which would have been in regular use in the average middle-class home:

Some households owned knife machines to clean cutlery but these were 'not fit to be trusted to careless girls' (from *The Book of the Home* vol. 2 p.19)

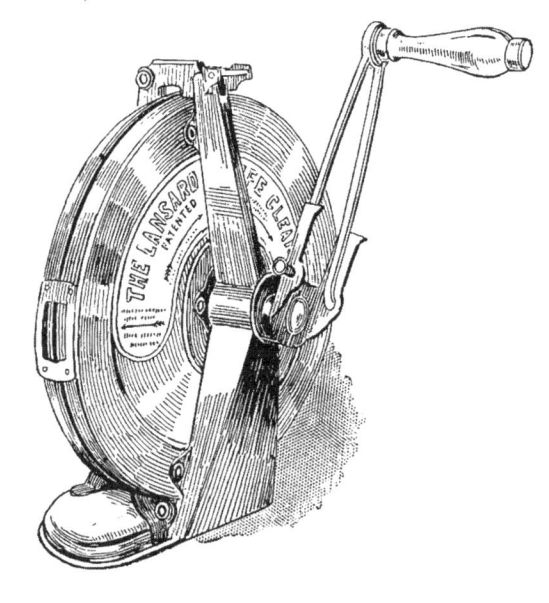

- polish, for floors, furniture, and metal/plate (Brasso and Silvo would be modern equivalents)

- knife powder, which was rubbed on knives to polish them
- hearthstone, a soft stone used for scouring
- blacking or black-lead, to add a deep lustre to iron cooking-ranges
- aluminium cleaner
- washing-up powder
- soap flakes
- soda
- household soap for cleaning: Lifebuoy and Sunlight were popular brands
- ammonia, a powerful-smelling liquid used for general cleaning
- window cleaner: Windolene was, and still is, a popular brand.

Most of these products would have been available at the local general shop, ironmonger, village stores or, for those households eligible for membership, the Army & Navy Stores, which was based in London but had branches in several cities including Portsmouth. Products such as Harpic (toilet cleaner), Brasso (brass polish) and Nixey's (black-lead) were very popular with housewives as they needed little or no prior preparation or mixing and were economical to use. Housewives were urged to buy the best quality they could afford as this 'paid' in the long run. In the late nineteenth century, products such as Colman's Starch was available either in boxes or loose, meaning that the shopkeeper kept a large container on hand and would scoop out the required quantity, much as sweet shops do today.[1]

Housewives or servants doing the cleaning in the early years of the twentieth century would have had access only to a more basic list, most likely bath brick (used for scouring), furniture polish, hearthstone, knife polish, soda and soft soap.

1 Morris p.6.

Brooke's Monkey Brand, a gritty abrasive soap, claimed to clean everything from stair-rods to marble (from *The London Illustrated News* March 1890)

Poorer families around the 1910s had hardly any money to spend on cleaning materials. A pound of soap for 2d, soda for 1d, and blacking for 1d were bought when they could be afforded, but even these tiny amounts of money were hard to spare when literally every penny had to do the work of two. At a time when 26 shillings was a basic week's wage for many working-class men, whose families could barely afford to pay the bills or put food on the table, it seems poignant that housewives were still laying out precious pennies just to keep their homes clean. The concept of 'respectability' was clearly deeply ingrained. Although keeping badly maintained or old houses clean was next to impossible, many housewives still wore themselves out with scrubbing and with putting a shine on the fender every day.

By 1913 things were not much better. Many working-class women were spending 2d a week on cleaning materials and wishing they could afford 6d. This enforced thriftiness sometimes backfired: a story was told (perhaps apocryphal, perhaps true) of one working-class woman who bought some inferior soda at a bargain price (it usually sold for 3d for three pounds), scrubbed, washed and cleaned her home with it, and ended up in the workhouse infirmary with blood poisoning, probably contracted via an infected wound. She was lucky to escape with her life.[2]

Just before the outbreak of World War II, social surveys revealed that a large number of families were living in abject poverty with minimal domestic facilities. This terse term could mean anything from having no hot water, no gas, no indoor plumbing and no bathroom, to no water on the premises, a toilet halfway down the garden (often shared with other families) and having to store coal in the food cupboard. One survey noted that a disproportionate amount of the weekly

2 Reeves 1913 (reprint 1979) p.60.

wage was spent on cleaning materials[3] and another showed that two bars of soap cost the same as 8oz of bacon (5½d),[4] highlighting a dilemma common to many housewives with insufficient money – whether to have a clean house or enough to eat. An investigation of slum life exposed the fact that some of London's worst slums were in areas such as Westminster, then the richest borough in England.[5]

An alternative to buying ready-made cleaning products was to make them at home, and advice books provided recipes for making polishes, scrubbing and scouring mixtures, and much else. Most brand-name cleaning products were cheap enough for the middle classes to buy but may have been more economical if made in bulk at home. Working-class women would almost certainly not have had time to mix and stir and would have had to eke out every last grain or scraping from the products they could afford to buy.

Here are some typical recipes dating from the 1860s to the 1930s:

- *cleaner for stone stairs*: a pound of pipemaker's clay (used to whiten) boiled with two pints of water, two pints of small beer (weak beer) and a small amount of stone-blue (a dye)[6]
- *French polish*: ¼ pint linseed oil, ¼ pint vinegar, 1oz spirits of salt, ½ oz muriatic antimony (perhaps to impart lustre), all shaken together[7]
- *brass cleaner*: 4oz soft soap and a 2d packet of rottenstone (used to impart lustre).[8] This mixture was still being recommended in the 1930s[9]
- *furniture polish*: a pint of linseed oil, 1oz spirits of wine (ordinary alcohol), 1oz vinegar, ½ oz butter of antimony (used to impart lustre)[10]

3 MGonigle 1936 table 34 p.228.
4 Rice 1939 (reprint 1981) p.171.
5 Chesterton 1936 p.151.
6 Rundell 1864 p.332.
7 Mercier (ed.) 1885 p.90.
8 Mercier (ed.) 1885 p.91.
9 Craig p.135.
10 *Dictionary of Daily Wants* 1861 p.451.

- *ammonia soap*: a pound of white soap, two gallons boiling water, two tablespoons turpentine, two gills liquid ammonia
- *soft soap*: a pound of stone potash per pound of fat, two gallons water – makes one barrel of soap[11]
- *Brunswick black for grates*: a pound of common asphaltum (added a deep black colour), $1/2$ pint linseed oil, two pints oil of turpentine[12]
- *plate powder*: 8oz powdered whiting (added a slightly abrasive texture), 3oz jeweller's rouge (used as a polish), methylated spirits to moisten.[13]

MANSION POLISH AND TEA LEAVES

Next to laundry work, floor-cleaning was probably one of the hardest housework jobs. One idea for stone, tiled or wooden floors was to put down used, slightly dampened, tea leaves (well rinsed to prevent tannin stains) and then sweep dust and tea leaves up together: the dust would stick to the tea leaves and the tea leaves would impart a gentle fragrance to the room. American housewives used torn-up pieces of newspaper sprinkled with water, and in Australia they spread fresh grass: it's debatable whether these methods saved time or labour but they do show a certain ingenuity. Sweeping a carpeted room was not simply a matter of sweeping, gathering the dust and moving on to the next job. The furniture was either hauled out of the room or moved to the centre of it, the tea leaves, paper or grass were strewn across the floorboards or carpet, a long-handled hair broom was used to brush the dust from the edges of the room towards the fireplace or open window, the furniture was replaced and the centre of the room was brushed in the same way. Finally the dust was collected with a dustpan and brush and removed for burning: in the late nineteenth century many

11 Kirk p.273.
12 Kirk p.274.
13 Craig p.141.

An immaculately dressed woman uses a carpet sweeper on a dining-room rug, presumably in a house not yet wired for electricity. This 1930s photograph shows the traditional use of a carpet-square in the centre of the room with highly polished wooden flooring visible around the edge (from the *Complete Illustrated Household Encyclopedia* opposite p.809)

people still saw dust as the source of germs and diseases.

Polished wooden floors were much prized in Edwardian times (or at least until servant-less women realised how hard it was to keep them looking immaculate). They were swept and dusted daily using a 'floor duster' and polished weekly. This could be done using a home-made polish (four ounces of shredded beeswax melted down with half a pint of turpentine) or a ready-made one, such as Ronuk or Jackson's. There was even a special implement called a floor polisher: the Ronuk company sold a similar long-handled polisher with a swivelling head so it could be used without having to shift furniture around.[14] Other firms made mops with oil-impregnated heads – O-Cedar is probably the most well known – that wiped up dirt and provided a shine, and other products included Mansion Wax Polish and Cardinal Polish (specifically for red tiles) made by Reckitt & Colman.[15]

By the 1930s those households that could afford them and were wired for electricity were beginning to buy vacuum cleaners and electric floor polishers to keep the house clean, and ideas in interior decor were tending towards the less cluttered and more carefully chosen domestic environment – although Reckitt & Colman's *Home Book* (published in the late 1930s) still recommended adding a handful of tea leaves to keep the dust down!

Scrubbing a room in the nineteenth century was particularly hard work (bearing in mind that most women wore corsets and were also dressed in fitted bodices, heavy long skirts, aprons, voluminous underclothes, and probably uncomfortable boots or shoes). Most houses did not have fitted carpets as they do today: carpet, if any, was confined to a square that fitted the centre of the room and left a bare polished area around the edges. It was fairly easy – although heavy and grimy

14 *Savings and Savoury Dishes*, back cover.
15 Cottington-Taylor (ed.) p.30.

- to remove, which was some small consolation, as the carpet had to be taken up every time the room was scrubbed out. Carpets were hauled outside, beaten on the washing line and left to air. An arm's span of floor was then wetted with warm soapy water, the scrubbing brush was soaped and the scrubbing began. Floorboards were scrubbed along the grain, the maid taking care not to get the wood too wet and changing the water when it got dirty (which meant trudging along the corridors and stairs to empty the bucket, refill it and bring it back to the room). Grease spots (common when people used candles to light themselves to bed) were removed by spreading a thick paste of fullers earth and water over the mark and scrubbing it off a couple of days later.

Stone or tiled floors, or floors covered with matting or linoleum, all needed specific care. Stone floors and stairs were cleaned in the same way as the front step, by rubbing with a brick or blue or gray stone, then wiping with a flannel; Indian matting, also known as rush matting, was washed *in situ* with salty water or taken up and scrubbed with soapy water; tiles were swept daily, and washed once or twice a week with soap and water, using Sapolio or Brooke's soap to remove stains. A light application of milk would bring up a polish if needed. Linoleum was washed only when necessary because it was easy to wash off the surface-pattern, although Greenwich linoleum, which was made with the pattern all the way through, could be washed with Brooke's soap and water. As well as milk, using an ounce of shredded

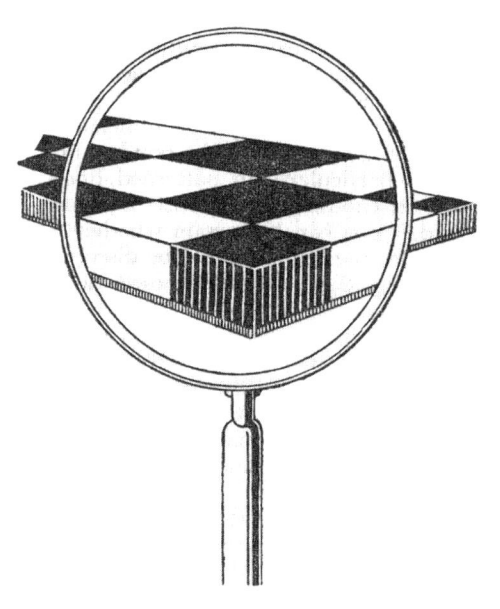

'Good linoleum seen through a magnifying glass. The design is inlaid and goes right through to the bottom' (from *The Book of Hints and Wrinkles* p.27)

The visiting Mrs Squirrel dispenses motherly housekeeping advice to Mrs Rabbit, while the youngest of the rabbit family attempts to use the mop, in this 1930s advertisement for Mansion Polish (from *The Home Book* p.136)

glue dissolved in a pint of boiling water, was another way to bring up a shine.

POTS AND PANS

Modern cooking utensils are so easy to clean that nearly every stain or burnt-on mark can be removed quickly and efficiently with a squirt of washing-up liquid and a sponge. It wasn't always so. Victorian instructions to servants included washing pans in very hot water, scrubbing them inside and out with sand, the rough texture of which removed food stains, rinsing them thoroughly and putting them to dry tilted up on their handles. Servants were often accused of low standards of hygiene, including being less than particular about the need to use clean cloths to wipe the pans. Victorian cooking utensils were made from iron, wrought iron, copper, pewter, enamel and tin, or block tin (thicker and more expensive than ordinary tin), tinned iron, cast iron, enamelled ironware, earthenware, or japanned (coated with a glossy varnish) and all required careful and specific cleaning and maintenance.

By the 1910s it was possible to buy iron pans with silicated linings that did not discolour food, and copper pans were beginning to replace steel and aluminium. Iron pans were very heavy, nickel was too expensive for anybody but the wealthy, and stoneware pans, clay terrines and earthenware casseroles were becoming popular, partly because the attractive new styles meant that they could be used from oven to table (which saved on washing up). This veritable explosion of choice came about partly because more households now had gas or electric ovens rather than the old coal ranges that sent coal-dust and soot everywhere and needed heavy pans to cope with the intense heat. One instruction for cleaning utensils used on the range began, rather depressingly, 'Scrape any soot off the

This 1930s advertisement for Min Cream features father and son discussing the best way to remove dirty fingermarks from the door – although 'it's easy with Min', the job will be left to 'Mother' to do (from *The Home Book* p.42)

"You rascal, what will your Mother say when she sees these dirty fingermarks on her enamel paint?"

"That's all right, Daddy. It's easy to clean them off with 'Min.' I've heard Mummy say so."

*

'**Min**' really is good for cleaning enamel paint. It is also splendid for giving a beautiful polish to all highly polished furniture. Use it and see.

M/AX/4

It's so much easier with

MIN CREAM

TINS 6d. & 1/-

FOR ALL HIGHLY POLISHED SURFACES

outside [of the pan] with an old knife'.[16]

Until the widespread adoption of non-stick and stainless-steel pans in the mid- to late-twentieth century, housewives had to be careful what cleaning products they used as each metal reacted differently, aluminium being especially temperamental. This is how pots and pans would have been cleaned from the 1860s onwards:

- *aluminium pans and utensils*: clean with hot soapy water and silver sand (a very fine-textured sand) to remove marks and burnt-on patches; soda was not used to clean aluminium because it left dark stains
- *brass and copper pans and jelly moulds*: reduce rottenstone (stone similar to pumice) to powder, sift it and mix with soft soap and oil of turpentine to a putty-like consistency so that it is very soft and pliable. Then wash off the pans with water and soda, rub them with fine brick-dust and vinegar, and finally polish with whiting (very finely crushed chalk). Brick-dust was almost certainly not scraped off the nearest brick wall: it was probably the dust-residue from bath-brick, which was a well-known cleaning product. Copper pans were treated with great care because of the fear of verdigris poisoning once the tinned lining began to disintegrate.
- *earthenware casseroles, marmites and dishes*: use hot water and a little soap
- *enamelled ironware vegetable dishes, pie dishes and soup ladles*: wash with hot water and soda then apply Brooke's soap or Sapolio; alternatively use salt, crushed eggshells or silver sand to remove marks
- *iron-lidded pans and double boilers*: wash in hot water and soda, rinse and dry thoroughly. Remove burnt patches

16 Kirk, p.314.

with boiling water and soda, then rub with fine sand
- *Japanned-ware such as flour bins*: wash in water just warm enough to dissolve grease (hot water caused cracks), wipe and sprinkle over a little flour to remove smears
- *pewter*: mix a small amount of good-quality powdered whiting with a drop of sweet oil (probably almond oil, as opposed to salad oil); rub it over then wipe clean; put some dry whiting in a small muslin bag and dust it over, then rub until bright with a dry leather (this prevented rust). This mixture was said to be good for both pewter porter pots and tin covers. In the 1860s inferior quality whiting was mixed with sand, which was a cheap way to bulk it out.

THE WONDERS OF RAW POTATO AND LEMON HUSKS

Before squirty bottles of washing-up liquid removed the slog from washing up, housewives scrubbed, rubbed, polished, scoured and wiped their way through a wide variety of materials from lemon husks to sand. As with nearly every activity in the home, washing up was a specialised business.

- *bottles*: cut a raw potato in pieces and put it in the bottle with a tablespoon of salt and two tablespoons of water; shake it up vigorously until clear, then rinse in fresh water
- *cake tins*: rub with sand after washing in hot water; brighten the outside with whiting and water
- *hair sieves*: scrub with soap and water and a soft brush
- *kitchen utensils*: rub with a flannel dipped in paraffin oil
- *knives*: remove stains from blades with a cut potato; wipe handles; stand blades in hot water (handles made in two pieces tended to separate if put into hot water) then

polish on a knife-board with fine bath-brick or knife-powder rubbed in lightly. This practice tended to wear the blades down so again, knives were handled with care. Some households owned knife machines but were advised that they 'require care and are not fit to be trusted to careless girls'[17] who inserted knives without first cleaning them. Brooke's soap or Sapolio on a flannel were also used to clean knives

- *metal-plate*: daily cleaning with soap and water. Once a week, rub with a rag dipped in a paste of whiting and water, rub off with a soft plate-brush and polish with a leather. Tarnished plate could be restored by rubbing it with hartshorn powder (made from ammonia) made into a paste with spirits of wine. Commercial plate-powders were said to contain quicksilver which was bad for silver and plated items (to say nothing of the health of the people handling and using such items)
- *tea services*: soda removed gilding so it was not used on decorated china: hot water and a flannel were used for any delicate pieces
- *sinks* were often fiddly to clean, especially if they had square corners or were made of porous material such as earthenware. 'Nothing indicates an untidy or careless worker more than a dirty and greasy sink,' said Florence Jack.[18]

UP AND DOWN THE GRAIN

Before melamine, granite, stainless steel and the huge variety of worktop materials that exist today and are wiped clean in seconds, there was wood. Endless hours and numberless fingernails were sacrificed to scrubbing wood in the nineteenth century, as servants and housewives toiled to clean

17 Stacpoole 1897 p.79.
18 Jack 1914 p.15.

By the 1920s households were beginning to buy electric vacuum cleaners, such as the Ediswan 'Little Glutton' (from *Punch* July 1923)

Sanpic disinfectant was promoted as 'non-poisonous' in this 1930s advertisement which featured modern young housewives (from *The Home Book* p.38)

wooden table-tops and floorboards, and to keep furniture and all the items of equipment known as 'turnery' in good condition. Wet wood splits and softens and eventually rots altogether, so sand (which, being abrasive, gradually imparts a bleached-looking silky-smooth surface to wood) was used for cleaning instead.

- *draining boards and tabletops*: in the nineteenth century, these were scrubbed with hot silver sand to whiten them
- *floorboards*: 'To give to Boards a beautiful Appearance' they were cleaned with soap and water and a brush, washed with a large sponge and warm water and dried with cloths, rubbing up and down the grain. Once a week they were scoured along the grain with hot sand and a strong brush.[19] Everyday cleaning was done by adding a handful of soda ('*more* is not of the least use, less will not help your cleaning')[20] to two gallons of hot water, getting down on hands and knees and scrubbing 'as far as the arm will reach'. Soft soap was added if the boards were greasy. To remove lamp-oil from floorboards, a mixture of pearl-ashes, water and unslacked lime (lime had to be handled with care as it was a poisonous substance and could cause burns to the eyes) was scrubbed into the stain. Before any scrubbing could take place the carpets and any small pieces of furniture had to be removed, so there would have been a lot of advance planning and shifting: the task had to be completed in the morning and would have been postponed if the weather turned wet or foggy – it was said to be unhealthy to sit in a room where the floorboards were only half dry, although this kind of thinking never seemed to extend to the servants who had to do the scrubbing

19 Rundell 1884 p.331.
20 Mercier (ed.) 1885 p.88.

- *doors*: along with painted woodwork such as skirting boards and mouldings, doors were included in the regular housework cycle. One nineteenth-century book advised using tepid water with Sunlight soap. Doors were cleaned from the bottom up so that dirty streaks did not run and mark the area that had already been cleaned.

FROM LABOUR-SAVING TO INSANITY

As long as servants were available to do the labouring, there was very little talk about the need to save either them or it. An advice book published in 1911 included a section on housekeeping without servants[21] but assumed that a 'daily' woman or the occasional charwoman would come in when needed, to do the hard work or 'the rough' as it was often known. In such cases the housekeeper was advised to look after her hands (wearing gloves for work and applying glycerine and rosewater afterwards to soften the skin – ladies were ladies, whatever unpleasant jobs they might have to do), to dress appropriately yet becomingly, to eat properly and to invest in as many labour-saving appliances as possible, including a carpet sweeper, knife cleaner, gas cooker and a mop for doing the washing up.

A combination of factors including the Great War, smaller houses, reduced income, and reluctance by servants – despite government pressure – to return to service after 1918, meant that many women found themselves taking their first real look around their own dark inconvenient kitchens full of strange implements known only to the departed cook, for the first time ever and realising that they were now in sole charge of the cooking, shopping, cleaning and housekeeping. Fortunately help was at hand, although the quality of it was sometimes a bit patchy. One post-war book began forlornly with a chapter

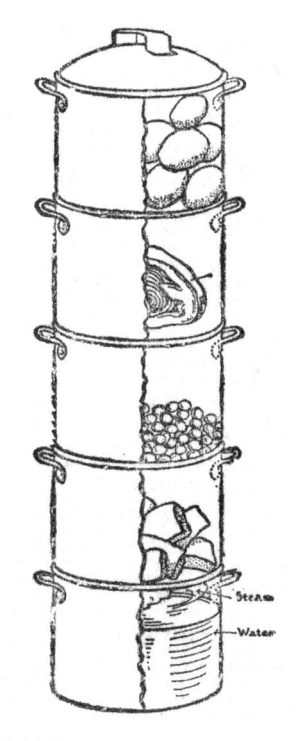

Multi-tiered steamers were said to be labour-saving: this tottering tower is described in a 1920s book as 'my favourite steamer' (from *Silvester's Senisble Cookery* p.28)

21 Jack 1911 p.56.

Glass-fronted cabinets kept everything visible and clean but free from dust, and were ideal for small kitchens (from *The Book of Hints and Wrinkles* p.162)

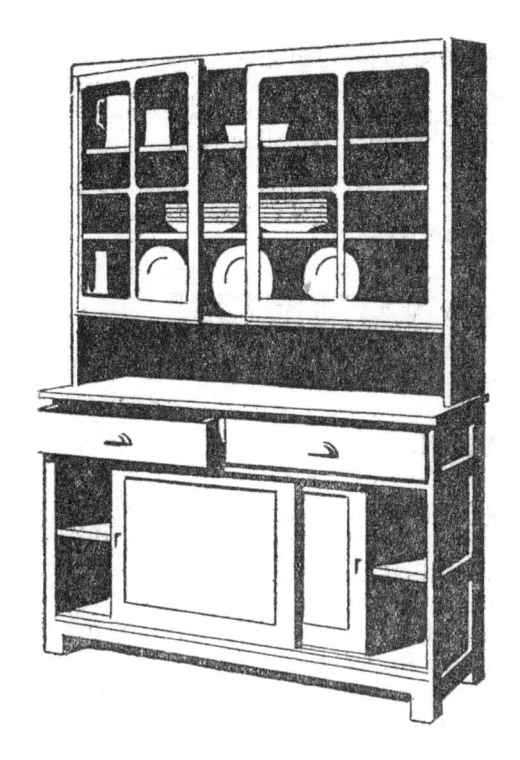

entitled 'Oh, dear!' and after a lament about rising costs and falling incomes proceeded to offer a list of not-very-useful hints including:

- tidy up last thing at night
- come down in a dressing gown 15 minutes before breakfast and put the kettle on
- wash up after breakfast.[22]

22 Silvester p.9.

This sort of approach was soon replaced by a more rational view of labour saving and ideas began to flow thick and fast. By the 1930s a basic list of labour-saving ideas would include:

- electric gadgets: floor polishers, irons, kettles, vacuum cleaners
- long-handled mops for floors
- gas or electric washing machine
- gas or electric refrigerator
- gas or electric stove with thermostat
- polish-impregnated gloves
- lacquer-coated brass taps and door fittings (no more brass cleaning)
- cooks' cabinets
- aluminium pans (lighter than iron and a better conductor of heat)
- multi-tiered steamers
- studded frying pans (fat was more easily distributed)
- stainless steel
- ice-cream freezers (no more hand cranking)
- tin-openers with scissor action (safer than the naked-blade monsters such as the old-fashioned bulls-head varieties)
- semi-circular pans, allowing two different vegetables to be cooked on one burner
- sinks made of teak (which was grease-proof and gentler on delicate china than earthenware), stainless steel, vitreous enamel, or Monel metal (a nickel/copper alloy)

A well-organised broom cupboard (from T*he Book of the Home* vol. 2 p.49)

Housewives were encouraged to decant dry groceries into co-ordinated tins (from the *Complete Illustrated Household Encyclopedia*, opposite p.297)

In addition, a wide variety of small handy gadgets was available, including kitchen tongs, pan lifters, spoon clips, pastry jaggers, butter curlers and egg slicers as well as a whole crop of knives for cutting grapefruit, tomatoes, potatoes, oranges and for preparing garnishes. House design was examined and technical plans, at this time more at home in architects' offices than in homemaking books, began to appear. Experts following American time-and-motion principles pursued housewives about their daily work, told them how to organise their kitchen work-surfaces and cupboards, and instructed hubby how to knock holes in the dining room/kitchen wall to make a service hatch to save constant to'ing and fro'ing. Dr Lillian Gilbreth (whose fame probably owes more to her having had 12 children and being immortalised in the Hollywood film

Cheaper by the Dozen) was one of many experts who investigated the effects of streamlining domestic work and cutting out pointless journeys across the kitchen.[23] Wheeled trolleys, rattling with stacked china, now wobbled along corridors more suited to stately processions by servants bearing heavy trays, and wooden draining boards were ripped out and replaced with new shiny stainless steel models.

Kitchens began to resemble operating theatres, white, shiny and clinical, and housewives were encouraged to decant dry groceries into co-ordinated tins (which apart from looking business-like also deterred pests which were fond of chewing into paper bags).

Now that it was so easy to have clean clothes and clean floors, women were encouraged to do the washing and the vacuuming more often: by the end of the 1930s it was said to be not unusual for housewives to be putting in a working day of 14 hours or more.[24] Housekeeping standards began to verge on the insane, and some books began to urge women not to become too house-proud in case their incessant fussing and tidying drove the family to seek its pleasures elsewhere. Sometimes women went literally mad from the strain of trying to keep the house clean: wives of miners and industrial workers, whose living conditions were often particularly difficult, were especially prone to this sad condition. Although there is no evidence that housewives actually put in regular 14-hour days, as recommended by some of the manuals from the 1930s, many people today will remember the immaculately pressed tablecloths, starched white sheets, gleaming furniture and slippery polished floors of their childhoods and recall that for many of them their view of a grandmother or mother was often little more than an upended bottom and a pair of reddened hands scrubbing away for dear life.

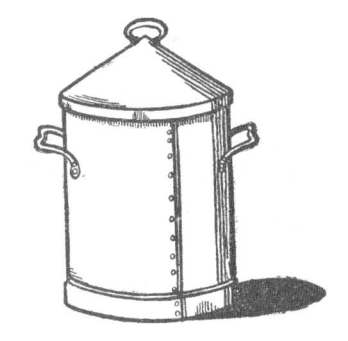

The galvanised 'sanitary dustbin' with its familiar domed lid and twin handles was in widespread use by the 1910s (from *Cookery for Every Household* p.15)

23 *Daily Mail*, 3 February 1954.
24 Craig pp.128-129.

This 1930s advertisement for Zebo fireplace polish stresses how easy it is to achieve a bright black gleam on the grate and hearth, and links this to the 'contentment' of the whole family (from *The Home Book* p.33)

Every eye is drawn to your fireplace

WHEN you and your friends settle round the fire, all eyes turn to the twinkling flames. The warm glow is reflected in the bright polish of the grate, on hearth and fender, and you are all content.

* * *

It is so easy to keep the grate sparkling. Zebo, the modern liquid grate polish, is quick, clean, and easy to use. You shake a little on to a cloth or brush, give the grate and sides of the fireback a brisk polish, and the whole fireplace sparkles! No elaborate preparations — you use Zebo straight from the tin. Zebo lasts a long time, too — it doesn't dry up in the tin. 4d., 6d. and 9d. — get a tin today.

A QUICK RUB OVER WITH

ZEBO

MAKES THE WHOLE FIREPLACE SPARKLE

RECKITT AND SONS
HULL AND LONDON

Elizabeth Craig, whose cookery books and housekeeping advice books were popular for over half a century, seemed particularly keen on a bewildering combination of labour-saving and complicated (not to say exhausting) timetables where the housewife was up at 7am, drawing curtains, opening windows and cleaning the dining-room and living-room before breakfast at 8.30am; out buying perishables (milk, fish etc) at 10am, home again making beds at 11am, cleaning the kitchen at 3pm (finding 30 minutes to attend to hair, hands and wardrobe – ladies, after all, must always remember that they are ladies), washing up and tidying the kitchen (for the third time in 24 hours), and finally collapsing into a chair at 9.30pm, having been on her feet for 14 hours and done all the things a maid would have done such as turning down beds and setting tea things out – with the one exception that a maid was paid for her labours and had regular time off, and housewives rarely did.[25]

WHEN DUSTBINS WERE FOR DUST

In the 1860s a 'dust-bin' or 'dust-hole' was defined as 'a place for containing the dust, and other refuse formed in carrying on the business of the house. It should, if possible, have a northern exposure and be furnished with a door, to exclude smells'.[26] Ideally houses had two places for dust and refuse: one for dust, ashes and vegetable peelings (to be converted into manure), the other, usually smaller, for broken crockery and glass (useful for adding 'crocks' to flower-pots or simply dug into a pit in the garden). Meat bones became smelly unless picked clean and washed thoroughly (or added to the stock pot), so were best thrown away with the ashes, and everything that went into the 'dust' pile was to be kept as dry as possible to avoid unpleasant smells.

By the 1890s a dustbin was 'a zinc pail or box, which can be

25 Craig pp.128-129.
26 *Dictionary of Daily Wants* 1861 p.390.

removed by the dustman and thoroughly emptied'.[27] It was ideally stored at least six feet from the house and was small enough to be regularly emptied and cleaned. This was done once or twice a week or even every day if the household was a large one. Vegetable oddments such as cabbage stalks and potato peelings (as well as used tea leaves not already removed by the cook to sell on) were now dried and burned in the kitchen.[28]

It was thought that dust harboured disease, so it was removed from the house as soon as the cleaning was done and quickly burned. By the 1910s the basic familiar 'sanitary dustbin' was in place for those rate-paying households that could afford them: made of galvanised iron, cylindrical in shape with a handle each side and with a domed lid. The noise made by the dustmen banging iron bins onto pavements was terrific, as many people will no doubt remember. The contents of the bins were taken to designated sites that were probably not much different to modern incinerators or waste-transfer stations. One of the many sights to be seen in Edwardian London was the huge 'dust destructor' at Shoreditch, where a massive incinerator consumed tons of refuse and was stoked by sweating workers black with dust.[29]

The tradition of burning whatever could be burned, using either the coal range in the kitchen or a domestic gas-fired incinerator in the garden and binning the rest, continued into recent times. The main difference now of course is that the galvanised iron bins have been superseded by the modern 'wheelie bins' supplied by local councils. Most urban communities now have fortnightly bin collections, and houses have either boxes or wheelie bins to store recyclables and kitchen refuse. Ironically we still refer to the bins as dustbins and the refuse collectors as dustbin men, even though dust is

27 Newsholme and Scott 1895 p.194.
28 Fairclough 1913 p.19.
29 Sims 1902 (reprint 1990) vol.3, p.32.

probably only a minute percentage of what is collected nowadays. Refuse is now rarely burned in the garden incinerator, indeed bonfires are now frowned upon outside specified times of day, and we seem to throw away amounts of food that would have horrified our thrifty forebears. This, together with the urban foxes and the plagues of maggots that infest our plastic bins in hot weather, are modern problems that perhaps would not have existed in earlier times once efficient sanitary conditions were put in place. Housekeeping standards were traditionally far higher than they are now, and every 'respectable' bin owner would have scrubbed out her dustbin with soda, disinfectant and hot water once a week or sprinkled chloride of lime inside, or even burned newspapers in it to sanitise it. However, the task of cleaning wheelie bins is still with us, and there are frequent complaints to the local authorities from people about the need for more frequent rubbish collections, especially in summer when bins packed with plastic bags attract flies.

SPRING CLEANING: A MILITARY OPERATION

Spring-cleaning was a job that was viewed with hilarity by those who didn't do it (chaos in the home, no dinner, husband disappearing out of the front door in high dudgeon, wife crying, dog and children covered in whitewash) or with stern resolve by those who did (making advance preparations, dovetailing all the different jobs and working in an organised methodical way). There were rational reasons for this annual assault: the hatching of moth eggs in May and June was excuse enough to link a special annual deep-clean with the removal of all traces of insect life and start the new season with a house that was fresh and bright and without all the marks and dirt associated with winter such as fusty rooms, tightly drawn curtains and coal fires.

'A room ready for the sweep' – with furniture and pictures covered with dustsheets, curtains removed and the rug rolled up (from *The Book of Hints and Wrinkles* p.116)

System was essential. First, the chimneys were cleaned, then any repainting, whitewashing and repapering was done, electrical items were overhauled, any major repairs were made to the house, and the stair carpet was taken up and beaten. A good supply of cleaning products had to be collected as no-one wanted to waste time buying or making whatever was missing: in the 1910s this would have included carbolic soap (a type of disinfectant), soft soap, beeswax, methylated spirit, ammonia and borax, plus dusters, brushes and a supply of cloths.

The actual process of spring cleaning could then begin, starting at the top of the house and working down to the bottom. In the 1910s a bedroom was spring-cleaned like this:

- remove the carpet or rugs and beat them well, take down the curtains, remove everything that can be removed and clean it, and cover what remains with dust-sheets
- thoroughly shake up the bedding (eiderdowns, pillows etc). Put new strips of calico around the sides of the mattress (to protect it from dirty marks – probably from tired maids rubbing past it in grubby aprons as they made or turned down beds). Alternatively send all the bedding away to the laundry or have it all washed at home
- sweep the walls using a duster tied over a broom, or rub the walls gently with stale bread or a lump of dough (bought from the baker and said to make less mess than bread)
- polish the fireplace and coat with Brunswick black (black paint: fire-surrounds treated this way would not have needed black-leading)
- clean paintwork using hot water, soap and a flannel (soda was not used because it stripped paint off wood – think what it did to human skin, as with the woman who contracted blood poisoning)
- clean the bedstead: wash the iron part with methylated spirit or paraffin, polish the brass with a leather, wipe over and polish the remainder
- scrub the floor and, when dry, replace everything that had been removed; put up the summer curtains, and heave a sigh of relief – one room is finished!

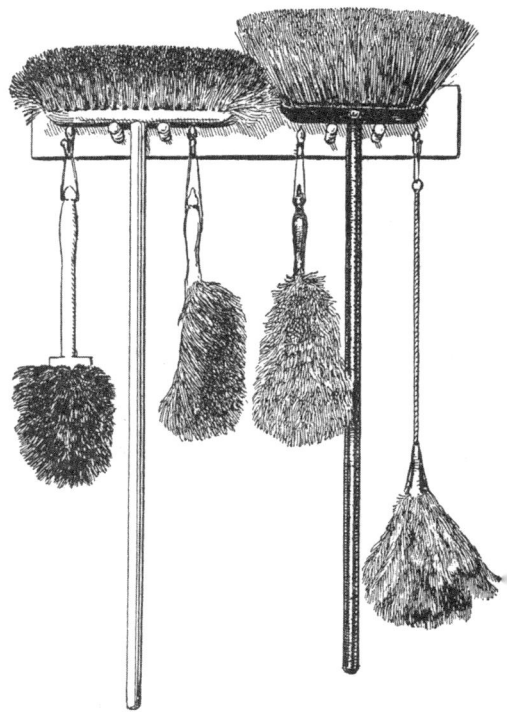

Advice books published in the 1910s recommended as many as 30 different brushes (from *The Book of the Home* vol. 2 p.47)

Even the most basic items were governed by a list of instructions regarding their proper cleaning. Marble fireplaces were cleaned with a paste made from equal parts of powdered pumice, chalk and washing soda mixed with water. The paste was applied, left for 24 hours and then removed with cold water. Oil paintings were rubbed with half a potato applied in a circular motion, followed by a sponge dipped in cold water (almost certainly damaging a few Old Masters in the process). Furniture polish was mixed this way:

- one pint of turpentine, half an ounce of camphor (a distinctive perfume), two ounces of beeswax shredded finely
- two parts of vinegar, two parts of linseed oil, one part spirits of wine.[30]

By the 1930s ideal housekeeping standards had reached the sort of level where spring cleaning was seen as unnecessary: houses were supposed to be kept in a state of scrupulous cleanliness at all times. Despite this, advice books still offered instructions such as packing the children off to friends over the Easter holidays, turning out cupboards, removing and shampooing carpets and stirring up cleaning materials such as these (admitted to be less effective than their proprietary alternatives, but a bit cheaper):

- *scrubbing mixture*: one pound each of soft soap, silver sand and coarse whitening plus two pints of water
- *brass polish*: four ounces whitening, one gill oleic acid (which may have thickened the mixture slightly) and paraffin oil to mix to a thin cream.

Shampooing a carpet 1930s style involved rubbing a damp

[30] Fairclough 1913 p.55.

Cardinal polish for red tiles, shown in this 1930s advertisement, was also used on front steps and paths (from *The Home Book* p.30)

cloth on carpet soap and then rubbing it over a small section of carpet, rinsing with a second cloth and rubbing it dry with a third cloth before moving on to the next section. To prevent becoming stranded in a damp corner it was best to start at the corner farthest from the door and work backwards on hands and knees towards the door. Another definition of the term 'shampooing' from the 1860s had no connection either with hair-washing or carpet-cleaning. It was a method of 'mechanical manipulation of the various parts of the body for the cure of disease', which appears to have been a form of what we would now call massage.[31]

Spring cleaning was, from contemporary accounts, fraught with perils of various kinds, but the worst and most heinous crime of all appears to have been that of unsettling the man of the house. One book advised that it was best not to do too much in one go, not to spare the housewife but because 'it is so depressing for hubby when he comes home from work', adding almost as an afterthought, 'besides being tiring and worrying for you'.[32] This particular book included a spring-cleaning timetable that was so brisk and relentless that it was a wonder the average housewife had any stamina left to prepare and cook the dinner, let alone eat it and wash up afterwards. The final day of the week's assault was Saturday (Monday: front bedroom, Tuesday; back bedroom or boxroom; Wednesday: bathroom, lavatory, landing; Thursday: staircase and hall; Friday: living room), and the kitchen and scullery were cleaned last of all:

- remove and wash the curtains
- clean and polish the furniture
- wipe down ceilings and walls, clean paintwork
- clean the gas stove (remove the burners, poke obstructions from the holes with a length of wire, wash

[31] *Dictionary of Daily Wants* 1861 p.901.
[32] *Every Woman's Book of Home-Making*, p.46.

the burners in hot soapy water and replace when dry, wipe the inside and leave to dry)
- scour the sink and draining board, chopping board, kitchen tabletop and other wooden surfaces
- clean the windows, wipe the tiles, scrub the floor, polish any metal tins etc
- remove the furniture outside, clean it, then replace it
- iron the curtains and re-hang them.

The annual spring-clean was also a time for stocktaking and replacement of anything that was worn out or broken. Inventories of china, linen and glass could be made or checked over, the numbers of dusters and cloths could be noted and replacements hunted down in sales, and perhaps even the annual budget could be overhauled.[33]

An interesting money-making sideline was suggested by Mrs Vince, an interior decorator in the 1920s. Pointing out that the average middle- or upper-class house contained a wide variety of high-maintenance textiles and materials such as cretonne (a heavy material used for upholstery and curtains), marble and ivory, she suggested that a 'furniture doctor' who made regular visits to houses might be a very good employment idea for someone with extensive knowledge of furnishings and paintings. Not only would she advise on the best way to clean items such as small marble figurines (Mrs Vince had been aghast to find that one household of her acquaintance had covered one such figurine with a coat of white paint rather than cleaning it with carbonate of soda), she would know how to clean expensive wallpapers, mend broken china and glass, repair furniture and look after all the small pieces and ornaments that abounded in middle- and upper-class houses that were otherwise left to the servants to look after.[34]

[33] See *Breadcrumbs and Banana Skins* for more information on budgets, Percival 2010.

[34] Vince 1923 p.166.

DOMESTIC SERVICE

Of course, not all housewives did their own scrubbing and polishing. Some households could afford to employ servants, and in the late nineteenth century a servant, even the most abject and bedraggled orphan or workhouse girl, was seen as a status symbol. Wages were almost certainly miniscule and working and living conditions probably horrible, although of course some employers treated their waifs well and did their best to look after them and teach them appropriate skills. Servants did the housework, cooked the meals, washed clothes, looked after the children, kept the garden up to scratch, grew the vegetables and flowers and mended the household linen. However, as far back as the 1890s, it is possible to detect a sense of dissatisfaction creeping into the well-ordered realms of domestic life. After the turn of the century, women themselves were also less keen to become domestics: between 1901 and 1911 the numbers of women in service dropped from 33 percent to 27 percent of the country's female workforce.[35]

This decline clearly had an impact on domestic life as 'mistresses' began to turn into 'housewives' who learned to cook and clean and generally take responsibility for their own households, and in doing so began to discover that many of the jobs traditionally done by servants were pointless and time-wasting. Large houses with vast expanses of polished wooden floors were less attractive when there was no-one to do the polishing, and dark basement kitchens that had been good enough for the servants suddenly began to look less appealing when the lady of the house was left to cook in it herself.

At this point in time the domestic literature began to encourage women to learn about the joys of the concept known as labour saving. Being a housewife was more than

---

35 Beddoe 1989 p.59.

Edwardian woman scrubbing

cooking the family's meals, for example: food had to be shopped for, stored, paid for, prepared and used up, and simultaneously the housewife had to answer the door, deal with tradesmen, shine up the front door brass and juggle the thousand-and-one tasks formerly done by the servants. Many cooks had been engaged as what was known as 'cook generals', a military-sounding term meaning that they were also paid to do the general work of the house when they were not actually doing the cooking, so the single-handed housewife whose cook had departed often had to learn to do a variety of jobs herself.

This gradual move away from servants to autonomy is therefore one of the pivotal points of domestic history. Servants fetched and carried, answered bells, carried letters on silver salvers (they were not supposed to hand anything directly to their employers – this was probably one way of maintaining distance between employer and employee), emptied slops, hauled coal, cooked the meals and kept the house clean and tidy, and when they moved on to other more rewarding and lucrative occupations, such as munitions work during the Great War, and shop or office work after it, things began to change in all sorts of ways undreamed of by their former employers.

According to various nineteenth century advice books, domestic service was a misunderstood profession that was unpopular with the very girls it sought to recruit to its ranks. Unfortunately the difficulties of reconciling the expectations and experiences of one social class with those of another have come down in history as an almost universal them-against-us battle of wills. Flora Thompson, in *Lark Rise to Candleford*, described the bewilderment, homesickness and alienation felt by young girls leaving home for their first job in service, and the contrast between their rural working-class origins and the often grand and sumptuous furnishings of their new surroundings. Although parlour maids were carefully trained and new maids were probably never let loose on anything valuable, it must have been intensely stressful for them until they learned the ins and outs of their new jobs.

The volume of information in old advice books on looking after elaborate and delicate furnishings and textiles indicates that servants had a lot of learning to do. And while larger establishments might have provided some anonymity for the new recruit, smaller households tended to employ only one servant and she may well have worked with her mistress rather than as part of a group. It would have been equally frustrating for the mistress of the house as she attempted to weld what must at times have felt like a sorry collection of individuals into a cohesive whole (although, as many people have commented, it would probably have been much easier if she'd done the whole lot herself).

Domestic service was also unpopular because it was thought to be a demeaning job. Fetching, carrying and cleaning were not glamorous when compared with shop or factory work (although work in shops and factories was extremely hard at this period in the late nineteenth to early twentieth century, with long hours and poor working conditions) but were seen, with no sense of irony, as good training for later married life. Nineteenth-century organisations such as The Girls' Friendly Society aimed to show domestic service in a positive light by pointing out that a live-in servant could save nearly all her wages, did not have to find her own meals or worry about accommodation, and could look forward to retirement and a happy old age secure in the knowledge that she was revered and esteemed by 'her family'. The writer of an article for the Society on the joys of domestic service compiled into a small volume uncompromisingly entitled *Work, and How To Do It: a Practical Guide To Girls* also dropped very heavy hints on the links between cleanliness and godliness, pointing out that God had his eye on young Jane's every move and would be down on her like a ton of bricks if she neglected her duties – 'Do you fancy that God is so great that He will not trouble Himself about housework, and cleanliness, and honesty? If you think so, you make a grand mistake'.[36]

By the 1890s the 'servant problem' was coming to a head. One writer of a book for new brides referred to 'the unexhilarating occupation of servant-hunting',[37] the unsavoury registry offices (similar to modern Job Centres but for servants and prospective employers) and the equally unsavoury attitudes and habits of some servants. It appears that domestic servants were becoming uppity and difficult. A servant-hunting bride was advised to reject any servant who said at interview that her previous employer drank because this usually meant that the servant herself had a drink problem. One advice book included a list of do's and don'ts for the prospective employer with more than a faint sense of resignation in instruction number five: 'Don't expect perfection in a servant. Perfect servants or perfect mistresses don't exist in this world'.[38]

What most writers agreed on was that servants should have their noses to the grindstone at all times during working hours. At the beginning of the twentieth century a house-parlourmaid might start her day's work at 6.30am by cleaning the drawing-room and morning-room, and end it at 10pm after serving dinner, clearing it away and doing the washing up. Time off was probably a matter between mistress and maid, which may well mean that it was not even compulsory before the Great War. In 1911 Florence Jack, author of *The Woman's Book*, advised that an afternoon or an evening once a week, and an afternoon and

36 Mercier (ed.) 1885 p.84.
37 Stacpoole 1897 p.55.
38 Stacpoole 1897 p.57.

Every piece of Brass in your home has a welcome for BRASSO

Let "Miss" Brasso get busy amongst your metal ware. She leaves a brilliant and lasting polish on all brass, copper, zinc, etc. The sure way to get this polish is to always use

BRASSO

there is nothing better

Obtainable everywhere in 3d., 5d., 9d. & 1/6 tins

RECKITT & SONS LTD., HULL
Makers of Robin Starch, Reckitt's Blue, &c.

When Blackleading use ZEBO

The use of 'Miss Brasso' in this 1922 advertisement not only feminises the product itself but implies that it is so easy to use that even a child could do the polishing

evening every other Sunday, plus a fortnight's annual holiday, was a reasonable compromise.[39] Female indoor servants worked extremely hard, and it was common for advice books to include timetables or Tables of Work both to ensure that all the housework was done regularly and no-one was slacking. A household with two servants might be organised like this:

- Servant 1 (cook)

Daily work: light kitchen fire on rising; sweep basement passage, hall and dining-room; clean knives and boots; clean steps and brasses (front door knocker, lock surround etc); dust dining-room; prepare family and kitchen breakfasts. After breakfast clear dining-room plates etc and wash up; tidy kitchen and compile shopping list for mistress (this was often the only time the mistress set foot in her own kitchen) answer hall door in morning; wash up after every meal; leave kitchen clean and tidy last thing at night.

'Special work': Monday: clean all windows except those in lobby or on staircase (the house-parlourmaid did these); Tuesday: polish all brasses, tin kitchen implements etc; Wednesday: turn out and clean the larder and pantries; Thursday: turn out and clean the hall and dining-room; Friday: turn out servants' room; Saturday: thoroughly clean the kitchen and basement in the morning; prepare all meals for Sunday in the afternoon.

- Servant 2 (house-parlourmaid)

Daily work: take early tea and hot water to bedrooms; sweep and dust stairs; lay parlour and kitchen breakfasts. After breakfast, clean the bedrooms and dust the drawing-room; set the table for luncheon/early dinner; clear luncheon things away and wash up the glass and silver; change dress to be ready to

---

39 Jack 1911 p.46.

answer door from 3pm onwards; take up afternoon tea; set the table for dinner, take hot water to the bedrooms; wait at the dinner table; wash up glass and silver; set the table for kitchen supper; arrange the bedrooms, emptying slops and filling hot water jars.

'Special work': Monday: turn out the best bedroom and count items for laundry; Tuesday: turn out one or two other bedrooms; Wednesday: turn out the drawing-room; Thursday: turn out the study and bathroom; clean the stair rods; Friday: clean the silver; turn out the housemaid's pantry and the china closet; Saturday: mend stockings, table linen, bed linen etc; count the laundry returned from wash (both servants were expected to wash their own cloths and dusters – 'It is very extravagant management to send these to the laundress' said Florence Stacpoole).[40]

This is clearly very hard work involving many hours of cleaning. Time off was shoehorned into these timetables, but not too much of it. Sundays were probably technically free (duties were not listed on the timetable) but would have included obligatory church attendance and it was very unlikely that the family would empty their own slops or do their own washing up: presumably the two servants had alternating time off so one of them was always on duty.

Another area of disagreement in the 1890s concerned servants' food. Some servants were reluctant to cook or eat the frozen meat from New Zealand that was becoming popular in England at this time, and refused to touch it: Florence Stacpoole was one writer who felt that such servants were far too fussy.[41] This might well have been because frozen meat was viewed with suspicion by the conservative British simply because it was 'foreign', but also because it took a little more preparation and slightly longer, slower cooking times than the everyday

40 Stacpoole 1897 p.161.
41 Stacpoole 1897 p.62.

English meat that most people were used to. The firm of Nelson Brothers imported frozen meat in the 1890s and, according to writer Mary Hooper, had huge refrigerated stores under Cannon Street Station and at Nelson's Wharf in Lambeth.[42]

The other problem was that some mistresses doled out the servants' food for them rather than leaving it for them to apportion. This could be solved by letting the servants prepare and serve their own dinners (good) or leaving them the leftovers (less good). Cold meat, which probably looked extremely unappetising in its leftover state, was particularly unpopular: providing a jar of pickles as accompaniment was said to make it more palatable, or letting the cook make mince, curry or rissoles out of it. Alternatively it was sometimes possible to assign a joint of meat such as a leg of pork or shoulder of mutton to the servants and leave them to do with it as they wished. They were allowed to have puddings, but nothing too fancy (one recipe for Zebra Pudding sounded far more interesting than it actually was: it was made with breadcrumbs, jam, an egg, and custard made from custard powder). All were rather redolent of thrift as they included leftovers such as jam-pot scrapings. Florence Stacpoole was at pains to point out that servants worked much more efficiently with good food and good nutrition, and recommended that the mistress of the house allocate watercress (a good source of iron), to the young women servants now and then, and that all the servants should be provided with a pot of jam or marmalade once or twice a month, plus a bloater, kipper or slice of bacon for breakfast, and 'a good piece of cheese' once a week.[43]

Yet another area of discord was that of 'allowances',

With so much scrubbing, polishing and sweeping, servants worked up quite an appetite – but all too often found that their meals consisted of leftovers

42 Hooper 1893 p.119.
43 Stacpoole 1897 p.64.

whereby servants were allocated a specific quantity of tea, sugar and so on per week. This meant that everyone had a fair(ish) share of the food, that the mistress could allocate her supplies accurately, and that pilfering or over-large helpings ultimately affected all the servants: any sugar stolen, for example, meant smaller helpings for everyone. An average weekly allowance per servant was four ounces of tea, eight ounces of butter and one pound of sugar (people ate much more sugar in the nineteenth century than we do today) and a third of a pint of milk a day.[44] It is easy to see why allowances were a problem. Not only did it reek of the workhouse system of doling out food, it also gave servants the feeling that they were not trusted. However, more autocratic domestic regimes had no trouble listing allowances: an 1899 guide to finding and employing servants gave this list:

- tea   one pound per servant per month
- sugar   two pounds per servant per month
- beer money   1s 6d – 2s 6d per servant per month.[45]

The drinking of beer was frowned upon, but rather than having the servants hang around public houses, they might have been allowed to buy bottles from the grocer as part of their allowance or have a gallon jar with a tap in the servants' quarters. In the 1870s Mrs Beeton felt that a pint of beer a day for women servants and a quart for men servants was adequate. Teetotal servants were by far the easiest to handle, partly because there was then no need to lock up the household's wines and spirits, but beer money was often given out: from 7d a week to 1s 6d a week in the 1890s.

Yet another source of servant dissatisfaction was that employers often forbade 'followers'. Girls who worked in shops

44 Stacpoole 1897 p.84.
45 *Duties of Servants* 1899 p.18.

This handsome sailor appears to be distracting the young servant from her duties in this advertisement for soap: employers often forbade 'followers' (from *The London Illustrated News* March 1890)

and factories had no such problems, but servants usually lived in their employers' houses and so were expected to follow the ground-rules, and this frequently meant that friends, especially men friends, were firmly discouraged.

One of the few plus-points about service appears to have been the flourishing but illicit trade in the sale of commodities such as used tea-leaves, rags and bottles to hawkers who called at back doors. Cook might have seen this as legitimate business – after all the household had no further use for them – but employers naturally resented such practices and the selling of 'perquisites' or 'perks' was much frowned on.[46]

At the beginning of the twentieth century, advice books were still trying to reconcile the differences between servants and employers. By now many people of the servant-keeping class were becoming preoccupied with the need to reduce expenses: 'A prudent mistress will supervise the various departments of the household, with a view to keeping a check upon her staff, and thereby repressing any apparent tendency to extravagance through carelessness, thoughtlessness, or wilfulness on their part', said the editor of the multi-part *Book of the Home* (1909).[47] Kitchen-based servants were said to be far too extravagant with bread and to waste cooking liquor and other leftovers, while the house-servants were accused of being too lavish with coal and firewood. Personality clashes were also blamed for domestic strife, and one advice book included an entire chapter (thirty-plus pages) on the way to make the household run smoothly and unobtrusively. The chapter was firmly entitled 'How to deal with servants', an approach that indicates that this writer knew exactly who should be in charge of domestic matters.[48] Moreover she was most insistent that the servants knew where they stood in the domestic hierarchy and that the mistress, whether she was newly

46 Peel 1906 p.53.
47 Humphry 1909 vol. 3, p.123.
48 Lees-Dods p.103.

married and timorous around her staff or experienced and confident, stood at the top of the hierarchy – or at least, in Mrs Beeton's term, she acted as steward for her husband and he stood firmly at the *very* top of the hierarchy.

Servants' duties became more defined at this period, with advice books spelling out very clearly exactly what functions they were supposed to perform. According to Mrs C.S. Peel, a 'tweeny' ('between maid', more often a very young and overworked general dogsbody at everyone's beck and call) was expected to clean the front doorstep, polish the hall brass, shake the hall mat and clean the hall; clean the boots and knives before breakfast; after breakfast clean the stairs, lobbies, lavatories, servants' rooms, nurseries and grates; after lunch do the washing up and clean the basement kitchen; get the servants' tea and wash up afterwards; dish up dinner and take the dishes to the dining-room door (no further because she was probably filthy by now and was not versed in the art of waiting at table anyway); wash up and tidy the kitchen; get kitchen supper and wash it up; and be in bed by 10.30pm at the latest ready to be back at work by 6.30am the next morning. The next sentence of the book, with no irony intended, reads 'It must be the care of the mistress that the "tweeny" is not overworked'.[49]

None of this means that all employers were sadists who bullied and starved their employees, or that all servants were fussy, light-fingered or work-shy. At a time when manual work was the only way to get work done and there were plenty of people to do it, working people expected to toil hard all their lives and the classes above them generally expected to be able to order them about in ways that we today would definitely not tolerate. Some writers of advice books advocated that mistresses should remain aloof from the servants, others felt

49 Peel 1906 p.74.

Only the most upmarket homes had a butler, so an endorsement of Silvo from such an 'expert' would have carried an air of authority (from *The Home Book* p.27)

Good silver's like a good character—it's got to be maintained. Take those spoons and forks, now. Bright as ever after many a year's service—and why? Because I've never used anything on them but Silvo.

SILVO
LIQUID SILVER POLISH

that a system of kindly yet detached guidance was sufficient. Some left it to the housekeeper to run things, and others felt that they should take their servants into their confidence and operate on a system of friendliness. It must have been very difficult whichever course was chosen. Living, as it were, with the servants underfoot all the time, meant that the servants saw their employers 'in every phase of character, in every style of humour, in every act of life'.[50] The best way to deal with such a degree of intimacy was to act with kindness and tolerance and hope to set a good example thereby. Early rising, method and punctuality were the way to good housekeeping, and the mistress was urged to ensure that the work ran like clockwork and that the servants always knew exactly what they were supposed to be doing.

The Great War ripped through the fabric of society, threw everything up in the air and turned everything on its head. Servants left domestic employment in droves for the munitions factories and all types of war work and when post-war the pieces began to settle again in a completely different pattern, a new way of thinking began to emerge from the ruins. According to one account of the period, some of the most basic rules of 'polite society' disappeared during the War: for instance, chaperones ceased to accompany young women to social gatherings because no-one wanted to have to stretch the already meagre meals any further to feed them.[51] Women were thus becoming accustomed to going about alone or with friends. Many women had already experienced personal freedom and financial independence in war-work and had no intention of being pushed back into their former lives, either as skivvies or pampered ladies of leisure.

Women servants were treated shamefully by the post-war government, which attempted to force former servants, on pain

50 *Enquire Within* 1910 p.316.
51 Peel 1929 pp.70-71.
52 Beddoe 1989 pp.48,13.

Covering the kitchen table with zinc was recommended as a labour-saving idea in the 1920s (from *Silvester's Sensible Cookery* p.12)

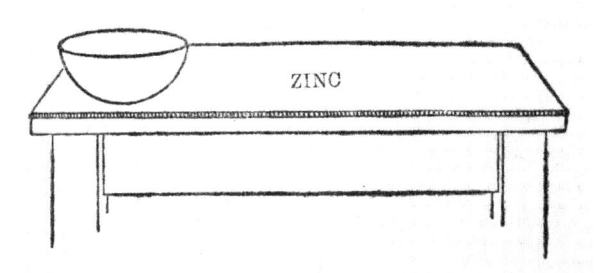

KITCHEN TABLE AND BASIN.

Best shaped Enamel Basin to buy—so nice for creaming margarine and sugar for mixing cakes or beating batters. Cover table with a large piece of zinc—a great labour saving device.

of losing unemployment benefit, to return to service.[52] In 1918 Clementina Black's book *A New Way of Housekeeping* put forward the idea of 'co-operative housekeeping', a system which in many ways was years ahead of its time in its ideas on labour-saving, streamlining of routine and ruthless elimination of pointless busywork.[53]

Because cooks and kitchen maids were strenuously resisting the recall to the kitchen, mistresses of middle-class houses found themselves having to either do their own cooking and cleaning or starve to death in unkempt houses. To assist them, a new breed of cookery and advice books began to take up the slack left by the departed or less loyal domestics. As Elizabeth Silvester said briskly 'Many of us have had to come out of our old groove and buy and cook for ourselves. The sooner we study the subject, and master it, the better for England – and our husbands'.[54] This bracing 'chin up, don't whine' approach, long popular in schoolgirl fiction, linked up the three strands of domesticity and 'good wives', the notion of

53 Black 1918.
54 Silvester p.v.

patriotism, and the idea of 'England'. The underlying message was that a resourceful patriotic wife would learn to cook and clean and run her house in a capable manner because that was what 'England' expected her to do: this was undoubtedly the sort of approach that would be known as the 'bulldog spirit' in World War II.

Fortunately for those members of the middle classes, who could afford it, help was at hand. A post-Great War edition of *The Daily Mail Cookery Book*. was years ahead of its time by describing a kitchen of the future organised for the single-handed housekeeper. It included moveable furniture, an easy-to-clean sink, an early example of a modern island unit (a table complete with a marble slab for pastry and a metal resting place for hot pans) and walls that could be hosed down; this all made for a state of hygiene and convenience that the average pre-war servant could only have dreamed of.[55]

Government policy ensured that domestic servants did not disappear after the Great War. Instead a new more flexible way of working began to evolve: servants lived in, worked 'by the day', came in part-time or perhaps occasionally to help with the spring cleaning, or were not employed at all. In many ways it seems as if they now had the upper hand; mistresses were instructed to entice them with attractive uniforms, paid holidays, regular time off, decent Christmas presents, lighter duties with whatever labour-saving appliances could be afforded, and comfortable accommodation – no more rows of beds crammed into airless attics or exhausted 'tweenies' falling into bed after a 16-hour day in an airless kitchen.

All in all, a housewife's job was hard work whether she employed servants or did the work of the house herself. Domestic technology was still in its infancy and nearly all household work was done by hand or with a few basic

---

55 Peel 1920.

implements such as brooms and mops, all of which took time and effort. Most tasks could be accomplished efficiently with a bit of prior organisation and the odd mental bribe such as a tea break, while 'big' projects such as spring-cleaning only came round once a year, and, if the house was particularly well organised, could be dispensed with completely. However there was one task that seemed to floor even the most organised and positive housewife, and that was doing the laundry.

CHAPTER TWO

WASH IT...

...Laundry work

The thought of wash-day seemed to fill even the most positive of domestic writers with gloom. Advice was often overlaid with bracing cheerfulness, and it's not hard to see why. Doing the washing, either at home or in a commercial laundry, was hot, wet, heavy work; the machinery was clumsy and frequently dangerous; the whole job took so long that there was often no time to do the cooking, and in wet weather the family might spend a week ducking under lines of drying clothes strung across every available space. No wonder one writer said that 'it is a well-known fact that washing under old-fashioned conditions is the hardest manual work that a woman is called upon to do'.[1]

Owners of modern, automatic, twenty-first century washing machines should count their blessings: our forebears did their washing in the river or used urine or paraffin to clean dirty clothes. The thought of washing clothes in urine (and other people's stale urine at that) might sound completely revolting but according to domestic historian Caroline Davidson, it was not unknown for nineteenth century householders to keep a communal barrel specifically for this purpose. Moreover both paraffin and petrol have been used for washing excessively dirty items – and fortunately, the fumes do wear off. Other wash-day hazards included getting your fingers crushed in wringers, being poisoned by oxalic acid and receiving electric shocks from primitive irons. Housewives may also have had to unpick the seams of their clothes before washing them, or make their own soap and starch from scratch. If lack of facilities or water made it impossible to do the washing at home, they might have used a public wash-house or sent large items such as sheets and tablecloths to a laundry.

Many Victorian working-class girls learned the theory and

---

1 Humphry 1909 p.141.

practice of laundry work in school and many more would have been trained by their mothers to help at home from a very young age. This chapter looks at the advice offered by housekeeping manuals and school textbooks to girls and women on the best way to tackle the washing – from the nineteenth century to the 1930s.

THE 15-STEP PROGRAMME

Nowadays we can toss a pile of clothes into the washing machine, add some powder, switch to the appropriate setting and go away secure in the knowledge that within an hour or so everything will be washed, rinsed and spun ready to hang on the line. Our Victorian forebears had to work through a long list of processes that included:

- removing stains
- repairing rips, sewing on buttons
- soaking
- first washing
- second washing
- boiling
- rinsing
- blueing (adding a small amount of blue dye to counteract the yellowing effects of soda and boiling and to make the white clothes look whiter)
- wringing
- drying
- damping and folding
- mangling
- starching
- ironing
- airing.

There was also a 'correct' order for washing the various items, such as:

- flannels, woollen and coloured articles
- muslin, lace and fine fabrics
- shirts, collars and cuffs (collars and cuffs were often detachable and therefore easier to keep clean; it was also cheaper to replace soiled collars and cuffs than to buy a whole new shirt)
- underclothes and bed-linen
- table linen
- coarse items (such as dusters and cloths).

To tackle all this washing required a whole arsenal of utensils. Here's a basic list:

- two large and one smaller washing tubs. A washing trough, oblong with a shelf for the soap, was more convenient than the round tubs, but was far more expensive, costing around £4 15s in the 1910s. Oak tubs cost 6s, zinc tubs cost between 2s 6d and 4s
- a couple of earthenware bowls for rinsing
- a 'copper' or washing boiler. This was a large cylindrical container, often made from copper – a good conductor of heat – and usually placed in a corner of the kitchen on a small brick plinth under which there was space for a fire. Sometimes coppers were built into a brick-faced furnace. The copper was filled with water (which had to be poured in and out by hand if the house had no mains water), the fire laid with coke, cinders or wood and then lit. Eventually the water became hot enough for the washing to be put in. The fire was also a handy place to

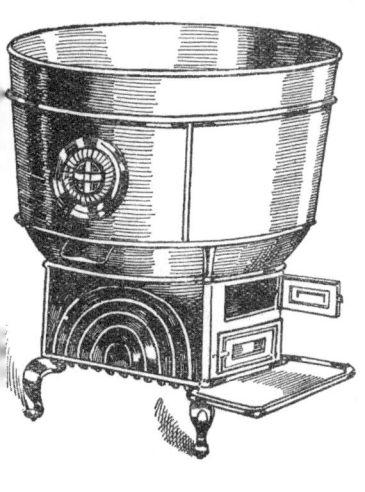

The open door at the base of this top-heavy looking washing boiler was where you put the fuel in to heat the water. The boiler, in use around 1900, was made of iron or copper (from *The Art and Practice of Laundry Work* p.46)

A purpose-built wringer and mangler, around 1900 (from *The Art and Practice of Laundry Work* p.37)

burn the kitchen rubbish. By 1909 a 'portable boiler' (with wheels and a small built-in fire space) was available. Copper boilers heated by gas were also available in the 1930s

- a copper stick, a long stout wooden stick for fishing up the washing and pushing it down under the water
- a washboard, a board made from wood, glass or zinc, usually with horizontally corrugated sides. The clothes

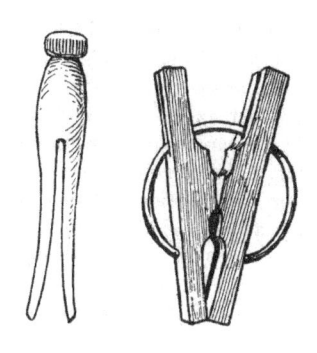

Wooden pegs from around 1900 (from *The Art and Practice of Laundry Work* p.45)

were rubbed up and down the ridges and cleaned by friction. Washboards were very hard on the knuckles but were cheap (1s 6d to 3s in the 1910s) and easy to store. In later years, they were to find a new lease of life as musical instruments in skiffle groups

- a dolly, also known as a punch or posser depending which area of the country you came from. This was a wooden pole with a crosspiece at the top for a handle and an arrangement – known as a 'peg', similar to a three or five-legged stool – at the base. It was twisted back and forth in a dolly-tub full of soapy water and dirty clothes. A dolly peg cost 1s 6d in the 1910s
- a dolly tub or barrel. Tubs were often galvanised and had ribbed interiors for greater friction. They cost between 3s and 5s in the 1910s
- a mangle or wringer (or both)
- a washing machine (A Vowel brand machine cost around £3 in the 1910s)
- clothes-lines, pegs and prop, when drying clothes outside. The line was made from either rope or wire and was wiped before every use. The prop was usually a long thick wooden pole with a v-shaped ridge cut out at the top. It was hooked under the line and hauled upright so that the washing caught the wind and larger items such as sheets did not drag on the ground
- a slatted pulley or clothes horse for indoor drying
- an ironing table. Most women used the kitchen table, suitably padded with old blankets, although ironing boards were becoming popular by the mid 1930s. There were also specialist items such as polishing-boards, shirt-boards and sleeve-boards which were in use by the 1910s
- irons. A number 6 flat iron – a standard everyday size of

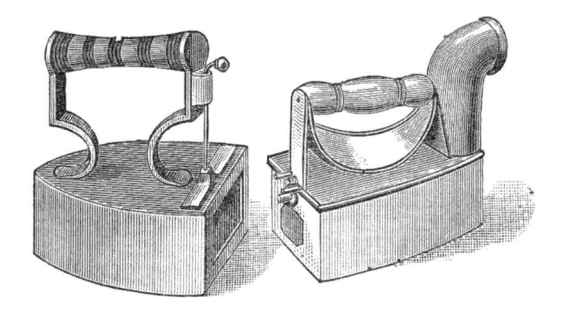

A box-iron and charcoal iron from the 1890s: the latter were said to be 'much used on the Continent' (from Domestic Economy p.240)

iron – cost 1s. Specialist items such as polishing-irons and goffering-irons were popular in the 1910s: a polishing iron cost 1s, a set of goffering tongs was 6d to 1s, a Dalli (Italian) iron cost 6s and the charcoal blocks used to heat them were 2½d per dozen. A lace punch cost 1s
- small sundries such as a soap dish, a bowl for starch, a knife and pan for making soap jelly, a clothes basket, a comb for fringes, spoons, measures, towels and soft rags.[2]

Then there were the stain removers such as methylated spirit, turpentine (which removed tar and paint), borax (used to soften water), soda (which also softened water as well as removing stains and softening grease-marks), petrol (which removed grease stains), chloride of lime (for stubborn stains on table linen), oxalic acid (for rust and ink stains), and a whole range of extras such as:

- vinegar and salt, which set colours and prevented them from running
- salts of lemon, salts of sorrel (both poisonous)
- gum arabic, for fabrics that needed only light stiffening

[2] Rankin pp.32-25.

- starch, in hot-water and cold-water varieties – for more heavy-duty stiffening
- permanganate of potash, which imparted a dark red-violet tint so was presumably used as a dye – it also dyed skin dark red-violet, so had to be used with care and removed with a solution of oxalic acid, which was poisonous. Wash-day was fraught with such hazards
- beeswax, for greasing irons, and white wax which was added to hot-water starch
- ammonia for softening water and also for removing grease
- blue, in rock or liquid form in the 1910s, for imparting a blue tint to white fabrics
- soap – brown, curd and soft
- water.

SOAP

In the past, water was rarely 'on tap' and soap was periodically taxed until 1853. Traditional methods of washing dirty clothes before piped water and affordable supplies of soap included:

- pounding them clean in the nearest source of running water, usually a river, using a flat, wooden, bat-shaped implement known as a beetle
- putting them in a tub of water and trampling heavily on them (very bad for the legs)
- using a bleach such as urine (ammonia is an efficient bleach)
- using lye (made by dripping water slowly through specific varieties of wood ash or the ash from burned ferns). Alternatively, plants such as soapwart (*saponaria officinalis*), also known as Bouncing Bet, made an

efficient lather and could also be used as a shampoo (Culpeper also recommended this versatile plant as a cure for gonorrhoea).[3]

If people had no spare clothes, no facilities for washing and no money – and thousands lived in the most abject poverty as recently as the 1930s – they simply went around dirty.

Soap came in many forms. There was laundry soap (made with ammonia), green soap, yellow soap, curd soap made from tallow (animal fat rendered down), gritty soap (popular brands such as Monkey and Sapolio were sold for cleaning saucepans – Sapolio is still sold in Peru and Chile), marine soap (prepared so it would raise a lather in sea water), as well as medicated toilet soap (with carbolic, iodine or mercury added – mercury is toxic), transparent toilet soap (Pear's is probably the best-known brand) and many varieties of toilet soap with added perfumes or scented oils. In the 1910s, soap cost:

- 4d per tablet for Pear's or scented varieties such as Vinolia
- 3d per pound for household carbolic soap such as Sunlight
- 4s per stone for household soap, which was often yellow. A stone (14 pounds) is a huge amount but as soap improved with age, especially if cut into small blocks, it would have been bought in bulk and stored until needed.[4]

Soap for washing clothes came either as boxes of flakes, such as the Lux and Rinso brands, or in solid bars such as Lifebuoy. Bar-soap could be grated into flakes or used whole: any leftover bits and pieces could be made into what was known as soap jelly. Bar-soap could be used medicinally, made from scratch at home, and even used to make more soap: it was therefore an

3   Culpeper p.337.
4   Lees-Dods p.196.

Economy, creamy suds, snowy-white clothes and no boiling are the qualities attributed to Rinso in this detail from a 1931 advertisement (from *Needlecraft*)

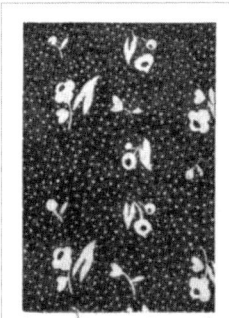

Lovely printed green silk washed 6 times in Lux—colors fresh and unfaded, like new.

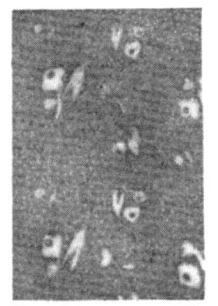

Duplicate silk washed 6 times in ordinary soap—colors faded and fabric worn out.

Her hair seemed to have new sunlight tones and her scalp was so clean and white. Now we all use Lux for shampoos."

If it's safe in water, it's just as safe in LUX

For all fine laundering
for washing dishes

This detail from a 1931 advertisement stresses how Lux cares for delicate fabrics (from *Needlecraft*)

extremely versatile and useful product. Women's magazines in the 1930s included advertisements extolling the virtues of the various brands available: Lux was popular in the UK, as its makers claimed it was the best for washing hand-knitted clothes, while in the US a veritable soap war raged – or foamed – between P&G (claimed to be the most economical), Rinso (said to be recommended by 40 washing-machine manufacturers) and Lux (said to be so gentle it could be used as a shampoo).[5] There was also a brisk trade in additives such as soda and borax for softening water and, in the early twentieth century, in the sale of water-softening treatment plants which could be fitted to the domestic water system. Such attachments were seen as status symbols in the 1930s. This was due to the fact that more soap was needed in hard-water areas, as hard water raised less lather, and housewives not unreasonably expected to see (as the advertisements invitingly pictured it) foaming suds when they did the washing.

5 *Good Needlework and Knitting Magazine* Jul 1938; *Needlecraft* Jun 1931.

SOAP JELLY

Soap jelly was usually freshly made for every wash-day. Any odds and ends of soap were shredded or chopped up, put into a pan and covered with hot water. This was pretty time-consuming as dried-up bits of soap are difficult to break up and very difficult to melt down. In addition, any wooden spoons used for stirring retained the smell of soap for evermore. Making and using soap jelly (which could also be used when washing the dishes, by putting it into a small, sieve-like container and swishing it through the water) not only used up ends of soap: it meant that the thrifty household could save a few pennies by reusing oddments that would otherwise have been thrown away.

THE WONDER OF SOAP

Soap manufacturers did their best to entice women to buy their products, making outrageous claims that, in a pre-Trading Standards era, owed little to reality and a lot to vivid imagination. Lever Brothers, who made Lifebuoy soap, produced a booklet extolling the apparently universal virtues of their product by claiming that it destroyed cholera, diphtheria and typhoid microbes within hours of application, and was also a handy thing to have around the house to flush drains and clean the larder.[6] Another use for the cleansing power of soap was probably less appreciated: curing constipation. When people ate lots of heavy starchy food and not enough fresh fruit and vegetables, constipation was a widespread concern and soap, with its undeniably efficient flushing qualities, was widely used in enemas both at home and in hospital. As Catherine Wood, lady superintendent at Great Ormond Street, put it with terse but honest accuracy, a pint of warm soapy water syringed into the rectum was guaranteed 'to excite the action of the bowels quickly'.[7]

6   *Secret of Health and Comfort* pp.63, 8-9.
7   Wood 1897 p.95.

MAKING SOAP AT HOME

Making soap at home seems to have been more of a necessity for women in the US than in Britain. People living on homesteads and farms in remote rural areas of America would have needed to be self-sufficient and to know how to make everyday items from scratch. Designer Lawrence Wright pointed out that soap had been made in Britain as far back as the fourteenth century and that a Soapmakers' Company was incorporated in 1738.[8] However, British advice manuals are mysteriously reticent on the subject of domestic soap-making. Three recipes appeared in the 23rd edition of *Tried Favourites*, including this one:

- boil up four and a half pints of water, six pounds of fat (unspecified) and three pounds of Black American Ashes for 15 minutes. Let it stand for 24 hours then boil for 10 minutes, stirring occasionally.[9]

A basic recipe for a smaller quantity (five pounds) of soap called for three pounds of clarified dripping. This would have been saved from a roasted joint of meat (some cookery books recommended pouring the dripping onto a basin and leaving it to harden, then spreading it on toast as a tasty teatime treat). Half a pound of caustic soda and one-and-a-half pints of water were added to the dripping.[10] Nineteenth-century American recipes, in contrast, called for huge amounts of raw materials which must have resulted in a mountain of soap, so the recipes may have been intended for farms. Mrs Abell, writing in the 1850s, recommended using six bushels of ashes and up to two gallons of lime; another recipe used 25 pounds of potash, three buckets of water and 20 pounds of grease.[11] The size and weight of the vessels used for mixing the ingredients can only be imagined, as can the rank smell of 20 pounds of grease left

[8] Wright 1960 (reprint 2000) p.240.
[9] Kirk p.273.
[10] *You & I Cookery Book* p.85.
[11] Abell 1852 (reprinted 2001) p.187.

over from cooking and stored for anything up to a year. Grease was particularly important: mutton or beef fat could be used or, if a lion happened to stroll by, a woman with soap on her mind may have reached automatically for a rifle. According to self-sufficiency expert John Seymour, lions have a layer of fat ideal for basic soap-making.[12]

Even without the odd passing lion, making soap was a great way to recycle and reuse many household oddments that would otherwise have been wasted, such as cooking fat or wood ashes from the fire (the ashes from coal fires, as used in many parts of Britain, were used on paths, in hen runs, and if they were particularly soft, for cleaning the inside of saucepans). The following method for making a soft soap for wash-day was demonstrated to American high-school students in the 1970s as part of their research into traditional crafts and skills practised by people living in the Appalachian mountains. First, the raw materials were assembled: wood ashes from the household fires; up to 15 pounds of grease from oddments of suet, bacon, grease, stubs of tallow candles etc, and any water used around the house (many rural areas did not have piped water, so every drop was precious). A 'hopper' – a box on legs similar in shape to a manger, with a run-off spout poised over a bucket – was made from offcuts of wood, lined with straw and filled with ashes. Water was poured slowly over the ashes, and the liquid (known as lye) that dripped into the bucket was poured into a big washpot containing the grease. This mixture was heated over a fire (the ashes from which would be saved to be used for the next session) until it took on the consistency of syrup.[13]

12 Seymour 1976 p.246.
13 Wigginton 1972 pp.151-158.

MAKING SOAP FROM SOAP

Although the obvious way to make soap from soap would be to melt it down, form it into bars or use it as soap jelly, there were recipes and hints galore in British advice manuals for making a few ingredients go a long way.[14] These included:

- melting half a pound of soap scraps, beating in three ounces of fine oatmeal, cooling slightly and adding a few drops of lavender or verbena, then rolling into small balls and leaving to harden
- shredding one pound of carbolic soap into a bowl, adding a 2d packet of carbosil (this may have been a powder or granule preparation) and six pints of boiling water, mixing it up and putting it into jars. The recipe adds approvingly that it is a 'most economical and satisfying recipe, as it makes quite fifteen pounds of soft soap'.[15]

FROM THE DOLLY TO THE WASHING MACHINE

The forerunner to the washing machine was the 'dolly', which was also known in different parts of the country as a 'punch' or 'posser'. The dolly – a wooden pole with three or five wooden prongs on the end – was twisted back and forth in a dolly-tub full of soapy water and dirty clothes, and this action, combined with the ribbed interior of the tub, swished the washing around with some success – and a lot of effort. A dolly was strongly made, took up much less space (and cost far less money) than the average contemporary washing machine and could easily be made from an old broom handle. They were much in use in households until way into the 1950s. A variation on the dolly was the 'chump', a solid rounded piece of wood with a groove cut front to back.

Delicate fabrics would not have lasted long under the

14 See Percival, *Breadcrumbs and Banana Skins*

15 *You & I Cookery Book* p.84.

Wooden Tub   Dolly Tub and Peg

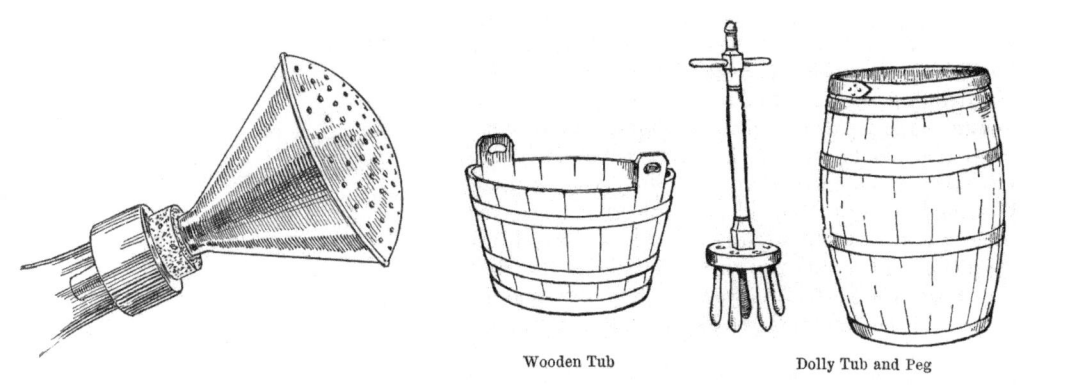

Above: A clothes sprinkler from the 1920s (from *The Book of the Home* vol. 2 p.71)

Above right: Instead of washing clothes by hand in a wooden tub (left) a dolly peg (centre) could be agitated in a tall wooden barrel, which avoided the housewife having to bend over (from *The Art and Practice of Laundry Work* p.29)

treatment meted out by a dolly, and a slightly different and definitely gentler manual device was the 'suction washer', which was a perforated metal cone on a handle. It was worked up and down in the soapy water without coming into contact with the clothes, and was popular in a small way into the 1920s: it even reappeared briefly in the late twentieth century in a Lakeland kitchenware catalogue. *The Home of To-day*, a housekeeping manual published in the mid 1930s, described an appliance made of galvanised iron in the shape of a large lidded bucket, with a cone-shaped sprinkler embedded in the base. Soapy water was poured in and brought to boiling point and the clothes then came into contact with jets of hot water that presumably forced the soapy water through and around the fabric. This method sounds extremely labour-intensive, as water had to be boiled in the appliance and there is no reference to its size, where it would stand while in use, or how the jets of water were directed at the clothes.

Other manual methods included the ribbed washboard and human muscle, whether legs (trampling the washing) or arms

Wash it...   Page 77 (beating it against stones). Such uncompromising treatment was not a problem for strong fabrics such as linen, but cotton would not stand up to such violence for long: this may have been one of the factors that spurred on the research into mechanised washing methods.[16]

References to mechanised washing machines for large-scale use exist as far back as the seventeenth century,[17] but home models took longer to appear. One machine, illustrated in an 1861 encyclopaedia, had a wringer and a sliding mangle-board. The washing area featured ribbed sides and a watertight lid to keep the steam in. The advantage of this was that steam apparently acted as a bleaching agent, freeing dirt from the clothes far more efficiently than friction alone would have done. One clear disadvantage was that whoever removed the lid caught an instant blast of trapped steam full in the face! However this model was said to take up very little space, to be very gentle with delicate fabrics such as muslin, and to be easy to use. The article skated quickly past the obvious details such as the fact that although there was a 'draw tap' to empty the tub (a large bowl would have been hastily put in place at this point to prevent a flood) the hot water had to be tipped in several times over, because manual machines such as these did not usually have heating or filling arrangements. This meant a lot of water had to be heated in advance, so the fire had to be kept well-stoked....which in turn meant that the temperature inside the house would have been unbearable in summer.

By the 1890s, models such as the Summerscales Household Washer were on the market. It had the ribbed interior, wringer and dolly arrangement of the 1861 model but had one handle instead of two, and cost between £3 18s and £5. As a working man on a good wage earned approximately £200 per year in the late 1890s this figure would have represented about three

16 See Malcolmson: *English Laundresses, A Social History*
17 See Hardyment: *From Mangle to Microwave, the Mechanization of Household Work*

The Summerscales' Household Washer, on the market around 1895, that enabled washing, wringing and mangling to be done all using one handle (from *Domestic Economy* p.230)

months' wages. A modern automatic washing machine costing approximately £300 represents an average week's wages today (2010-2011 figures).

The machines of this era still look nothing like our modern ones and, as each model had different features, it must have been very difficult to decide which to buy. There were machines with smooth or grooved inner surfaces; revolving or rocking tubs; friction or suction motion; and reversible or non-reversible motion. The only feature in common was that they were all manual, generally worked by a handle attached to a wheel (the 'Dolly' washer was rocked back and forth by a wooden bar, which must have meant the person using it was leaning at a very uncomfortable angle), and, inevitably, they were all expensive, costing between three and five guineas.

The concept of labour-saving began to creep into the public eye after the Great War, and by the 1920s a logical offshoot of this idea ushered in a period of multi-use appliances and furniture. There were grandfather clocks that doubled as drinks bars, bookcases that held coal, and kitchen cabinets that did pretty well everything except make a cup of tea. An ingenious combination from the 1920s was the Pioneer Chain Driven Mangle. To our modern health-and-safety-informed eyes this machine looks lethal – the wheel that turned the mangle was inches away from an exposed chain and probably seconds away from chopped-off fingers – but it came with a hinged piece of wood that covered the whole unit (albeit with a slit at one edge to accommodate the wheel) and turned it into a handy table top – a dual-purpose tool that was ideal for a small kitchen.[18]

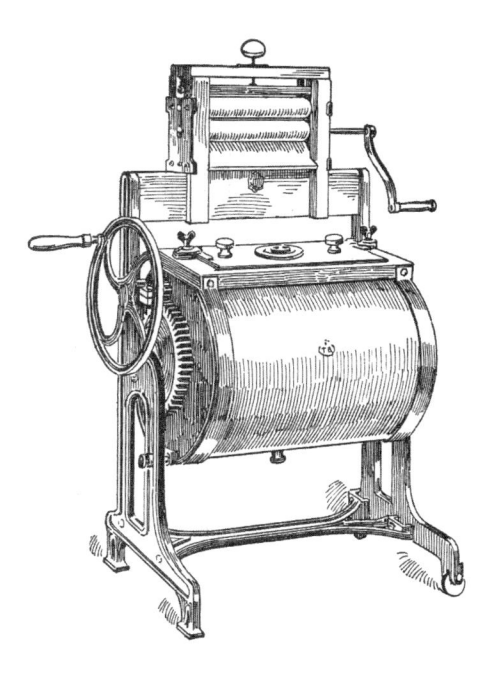

The Vowel Ito model had an inner grooved surface and cost £3 5s in 1909 (from *The Book of the Home* vol. 3 p.142)

18 Bateman p.31.

Electric washing machines 'have robbed washday of its terrors', according to this 1930s advice book (from the *Complete Illustrated Household Encyclopedia* opposite p.809)

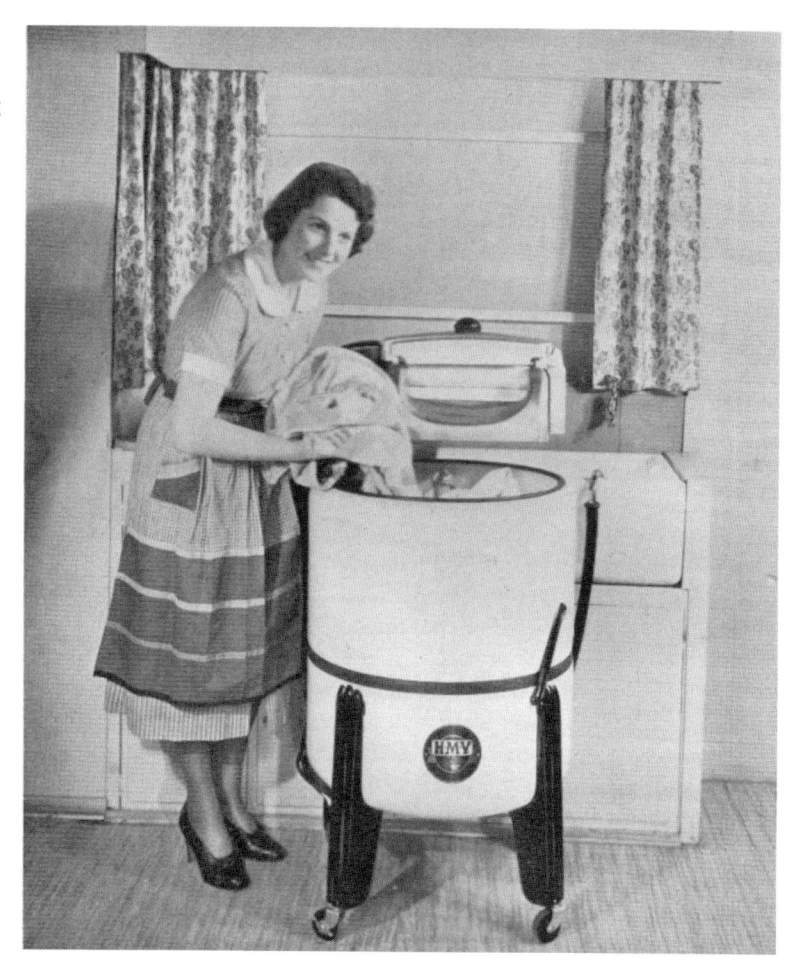

Advertising copy made the most of the fact that wash-day was universally loathed. Appliances were advertised as being very quiet in use (housewives were popularly thought to be irritable on laundry day), easy to operate, gentle on fabric, economical – a week's washing done in an hour and costing 3d – and the all-round answer to a housewife's prayers. As a rule they still had to be filled and emptied by hand, but by the 1930s gas or electric models were available (if the house had gas laid on or was wired for electricity). The gas-operated machines could either heat water direct from the tap, or heat up the water once it was in the tub.

DRYING AND MANGLING

Drying the washing in pre-tumble-dryer days was a major problem in most households. Line drying was the ideal method, but if there was no washing line women hung wet clothes on bushes or spread them on the ground. Drying washing indoors in wet weather was even more difficult. Before central heating was widely available, the traditional method of heating the British house was by wood or coal fires, or by coal ranges. It was therefore very difficult to dry anything quickly. Fabrics such as linen and serge were thick and heavy when wet and took a long time to dry. Wet washing festooned around a room was unpleasant, absorbed cooking smells and attracted coal smuts. Drying it around the fire was only a safe option if a sturdy fireguard was in place, and foldable clothes-horses, which were easy to store, took up a lot of space in use. Special ceiling-mounted racks were ideal as the washing could be arranged on the rows of slats and the whole device hauled up on pulleys high out of the way.

The frequent colds and chills of the working classes were blamed on constant exposure to wet washing being dried

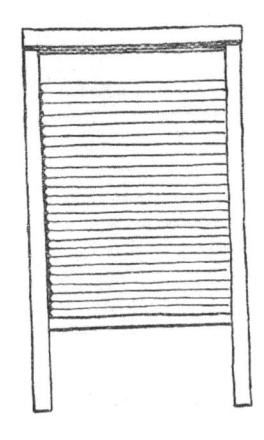

Clothes were rubbed up and down on wooden washboards (from *The Art and Practice of Laundry Work* p.35)

indoors,[19] and there are accounts of miners' wives having to dry their husband's working clothes overnight because they only had one coat and one pair of trousers. Sometimes children had to stay in bed because their only set of clothes was in the wash. And sometimes there was simply nowhere indoors to dry the washing and no back yard or garden either. Then it had to be hung outside in the public alleyway between two rows of houses where it would take its chances with carts and passers-by.

One of the hardest parts of wash-day (apart, of course, from hot water, swollen red hands, scraped knuckles, soaking-wet clothes, possible electrocution from dodgy electric motors and handling dubious chemicals) was expelling the water from the washed clothes. Washerwomen and laundry maids were traditionally strong-built and burly because wet washing was very heavy. Lifting and emptying wooden tubs full of water, scrubbing out coppers, hauling loaded baskets down the garden and hanging huge pieces of linen on the line were not jobs for a small or slightly-built woman – yet laundry work was, mysteriously, almost exclusively a female preserve, with the exception of some male machine-operators working in commercial laundries.

While some fabrics could be twisted between the hands to wring them out, others needed more care: wool was liable to pull out of shape if it was wrung with too much muscle behind it, and delicate fabrics would rip or split. To counteract this, various wringing machines were available by the 1860s. Although some contemporary sources used the terms 'wringer' and 'mangle' interchangeably for any appliance with rollers and a wheel, there were differences between them. Wringers were used early in the washing process to expel water from the wet clothes, and mangles were used to smooth and press the

[19] Bell 1907 (reprint 1985) p.232.

clothes prior to ironing: in reality, however, one machine could do both jobs. Floor-standing models, such as the one illustrated, were made from cast iron and were very heavy, but lighter wringers with india-rubber rollers were available by the 1890s: costing a few shillings, they could be attached to the washing tub or washing machine.

The technique of wringing was fairly straightforward: the clothes were folded along the selvedges then inserted between the rollers, the wheel was turned, the water was wrung out into a bucket and the clothes were put ready to dry. Pillowcases were inserted closed-end-first so the sudden ejection of water did not split the seams and douse the worker in hot water. Delicate fabrics such as muslin were not put through the

Above left: Wringing the washing in a Vowel machine, around 1900 (from *The Art and Practice of Laundry Work* p.35)

Above right: The Dolly model, from 1909, featured a 'dasher' that was cranked backwards and forwards (from *The Book of the Home* vol. 3 p.142)

wringing machine: instead they were squeezed gently and folded in towels before being wrung by hand.

Mangling, on the other hand, required some skill and patience as every item had to be prepared in advance by careful folding. Clothes at this time were fastened by rows of tiny buttons or sets of tapes that tied together like the two ends of string and all these had to be folded inside the garment to prevent breakages or rips. All edges were butted together, the selvedges lined up and the garment pulled carefully into shape. Clothes had to be cool, as heat ruined the india-rubber rollers (probably a fortunate thing for the person feeding them through). Sheets, towels and aprons were ironed damp, small items were mangled together and large ones individually. For best results, one person fed the items through and kept them straight while the other turned the handle. Children were often roped in to be handle-turners, and in *Our Mutual Friend* by Charles Dickens there is a reference to a child whose mother has died, wishing sorrowfully that he'd turned her mangle more willingly when she was alive.

Wringers and mangles were the predecessors to spin dryers and tumble dryers in that they expelled water and saved the housewife or laundry-maid hours of labour. Their overall look did not alter much: the Bradford Acorn wringer mentioned in a 1909 book was attached to a washing tray; an almost identical one appears in a 1927 book and again in the 1930s, though this time attached to a gas washing machine. Acme wringers appear to have been particularly hard-wearing and popular well into the 1960s, and indeed wringers in general were incredibly sturdy machines, working for years with no problems as long as the rollers were kept in good condition and the tension screw used properly.

By the 1930s the humble clothes-horse had blossomed from

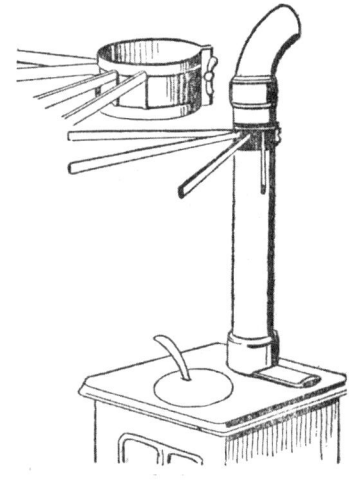

the basic two-armed model hinged in the middle into a variety of inventive shapes made to suit different spaces. There was the 'radial' for small items, the 'tree' with branches that folded flat when not in use, the extendable 'sliding' which fitted round a fireplace, and a model that fitted to a mantelpiece and swung out over the fire, ideal for a small room or a single person. There was even a cooking stove with a glass-fronted space that could be used either for airing clothes or warming plates.[20]

However, a more permanent place for putting clothes to air was the still-familiar and still-useful airing cupboard. A similar arrangement available in the 1930s was the gas-heated drying cabinet. One example was described as having a white enamelled exterior lined with asbestos, with rails inside that could be drawn in and out. The cabinet was said to dry a week's washing for seven people in three hours using 4½d worth of

Above left: The Premier box mangle for professional use in big private houses or in institutions (from *The Art and Practice of Laundry Work* p.39)

Above right: Fixing metal rods onto the boiler-pipe enabled it to be used to air dishcloths (from *The Book of Hints and Wrinkles* p.183)

20 *Home of To-Day* p.108.

gas. It would almost certainly have taken up a lot of space and was probably an expensive item to buy but, as the book pointed out, it would have been very useful in those households where all the washing was done at home.[21] Similar drying cabinets were still in use into the 1960s: people might remember the free-standing appliances known as Flatleys that ate electricity at a great rate, or the drying cabinets built into some 1960s flats. A modern version of the Flatley has recently appeared on the market: Lakeland, the kitchenware firm, has introduced a model called the Dry Soon Drying Pod.

A WELL-STARCHED SHIRT

It was seen as a degree of housewifely excellence to be a good starcher. Well-starched fabric was stiff and glossy and would repel dust and dirt, whereas a badly starched surface was bubbly or lumpy. Beginners practised on small items such as handkerchiefs and tray-cloths, then progressed to aprons, tablecloths, table napkins and shirts. Starch was made from tapioca, arrowroot, barley, acorns, oats, rye, buckwheat, wheat, potato, maize or rice, and was as prone to adulteration as food products were (flour, various powders and wax were well-known adulterants in the 1890s).[22] Robin was a popular brand of starch over many years and is still available today as a spray – far easier than fiddling about with the raw ingredients.

The most popular starch in the 1890s was made from rice, as wheat starch could leave marks on the linen after ironing. Hot starch was made by blending four ounces of starch with

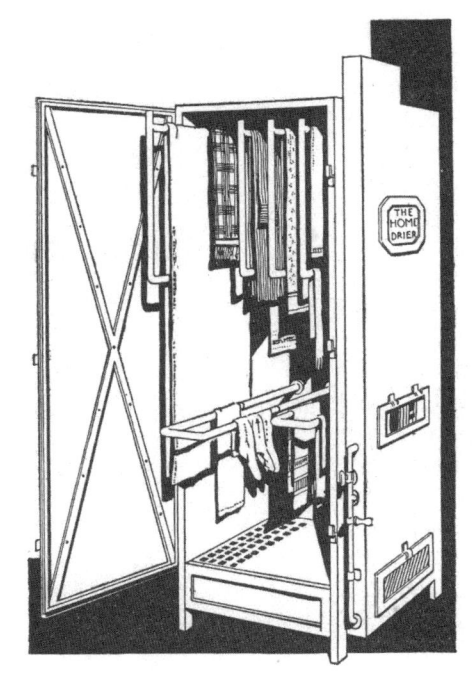

The 'Eco-Dry' drying cabinet from the 1920s: some cabinets were powered by gas (from *The Book of the Home* vol. 2 p.70)

21 Simpson 1934 p.264.
22 Newsholme & Scott 1895 p.237.

four tablespoons of cold water, then pouring over four pints of boiling water, stirring all the time (this is another reason why laundry-maids were strong: pouring half a gallon of boiling water and stirring at the same time is no mean feat of strength). A small amount of paraffin or turpentine, a lump of sugar or a pinch of borax added to the mixture would prevent the iron sticking and also added a gloss to the linen, as would a small piece of candle. The starch was ready to use once it was the consistency of thin paste, had turned semi-transparent and was free from lumps.

Cold starch was made using cold instead of boiling water. Items such as shirts, collars and cuffs were cold-water starched, as the heat from the iron 'cooked' the starch and made it stiff; dresses, aprons, curtains and so on were hot-water starched as the starch had already been 'cooked'. Coloured starch was available for dyeing muslin curtains but its yellow tint was not very popular as most people preferred the natural colour of lace.

Organisation was key: the bowl of starch was placed next to the ironing board and the items to be starched were dipped into the bowl in strict order: collars, cuffs and shirts were done first as traditionally they were stiffly starched; then table linen and skirts after that. Body linen, otherwise known as underwear, was rubbed well with starch (imagine the scratchiness!). More delicate fabrics such as muslin were clapped between the hands and shaken about before being rolled in a cloth to remove excess starch. Even more delicate fabrics were gently stiffened up with a weak solution of isinglass (a gelatine obtained from sturgeon) and water.[23] Very fragile or delicate fabrics such as silk and lace could be treated with a solution of gum water (two ounces of gum arabic washed with cold water with one pint of boiling water poured over) to stiffen the fabric without making it too resistant.

23 Newsholme & Scott 1895 p.238.

Instructions for ironing 'body linen' (from *Practical Laundry Work* p.89)

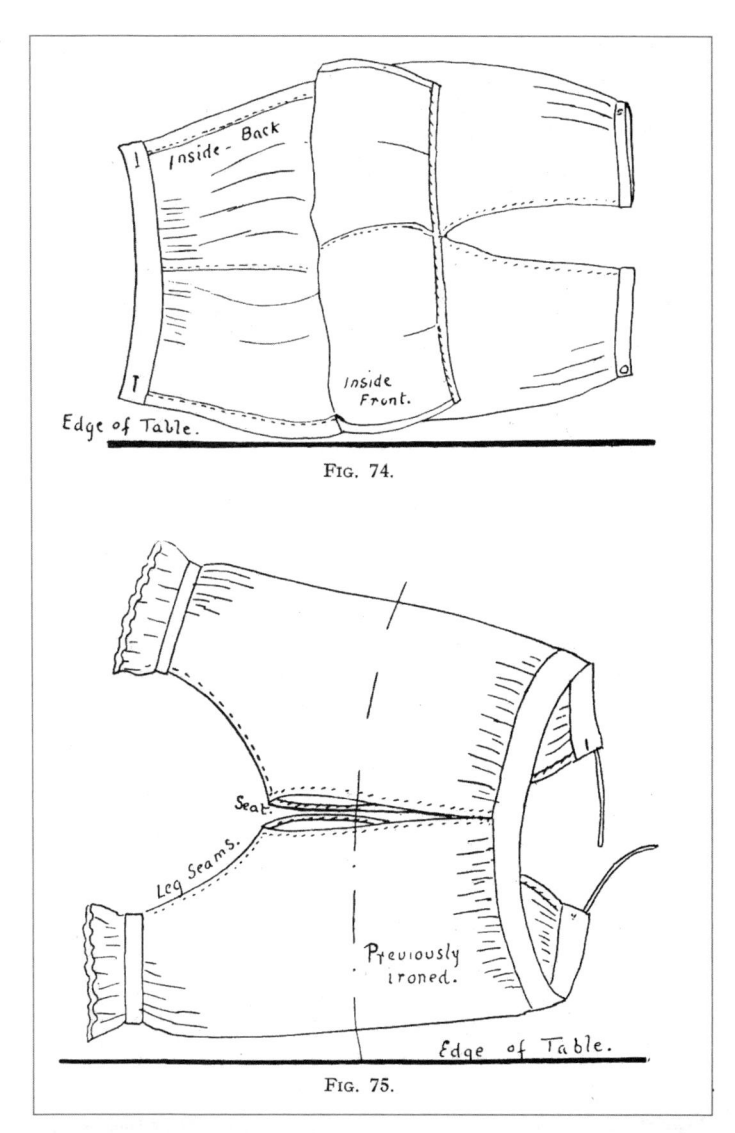

Fig. 74.

Fig. 75.

Shirt-fronts were also routinely 'glossed' or polished. After starching they were damped down with a clean wet cloth and the front of the shirt was rubbed over with a special iron known as a glossing or polishing iron: this produced the shiny, almost glazed, appearance that was much admired in Victorian times, not to mention the exaggeratedly upright stance of the Victorian gentlemen who wore the shirt.

A shirt was starched this way:

- rub a handful of starch into the shirt front, avoiding all other parts
- squeeze it to distribute the starch evenly
- place a clean handkerchief over the starched front and roll it up to be ironed
- dip the collar and cuffs in the starch and repeat the process.

During the Great War, a restriction was placed on the use of starch in laundries because potatoes, from which starch was made, were scarce. The cost of washing doubled after the war as prices rose in almost every area of life, due partly to the shortage of raw materials,[24] but starching continued to be an important part of the washing routine right into the 1960s.[25]

DASHING AWAY WITH THE SMOOTHING IRON

Modern electric irons are cheap, reliable and well made. They heat up in seconds, are safe, light and comfortable to use, and come in a range of attractive colours. In the 1930s, housewives had fewer options but could choose between flat-irons (heated by fire), box-irons (old fashioned in the 1930s but useful in houses with neither gas nor electricity), irons heated with

24 Peel 1929 pp.94, 185.
25 *Good Housekeeping Encyclopedia* 1951 (reprint 1967) pp.424-425.

Fig. 6.

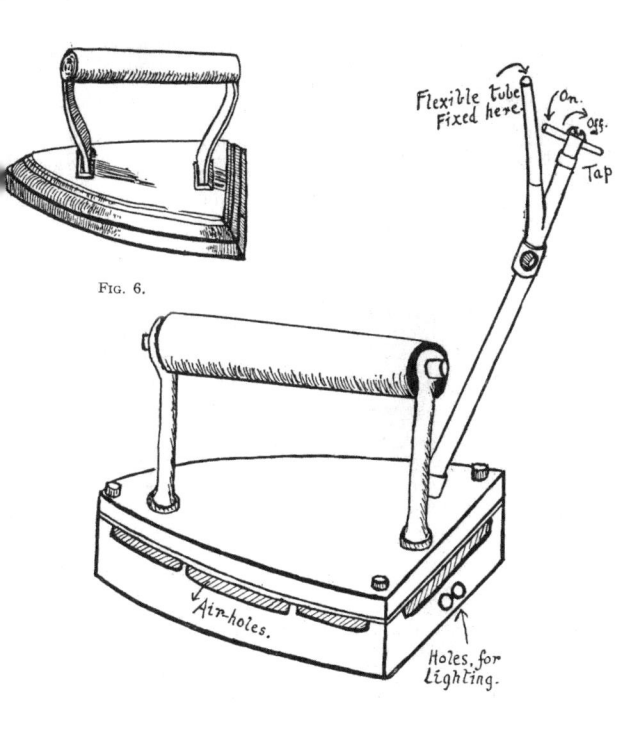

A flat-iron (top) and a gas iron, from around 1900 (from *Practical Laundry Work* p.25)

methylated spirit; gas or electric irons, and also specialist goffering and polishing irons. Households with a great deal of ironing to do might have invested in an electric roller ironing machine, also known as a calender machine. This device ironed several items at once, with the clothes arranged on a cylinder between a padded roller and a heated metal top-section. When the cylinder revolved, the metal lid closed down around it and pressed the clothes uniformly flat. Such machines were probably more used in laundries, but larger private houses with dedicated laundry facilities may well have experimented with them.

Even as early as the 1860s, women had the choice of box-irons, flat-irons and Italian irons for everyday use. All irons needed careful handling: there were no temperature controls, which meant that an iron taken straight from the fire was red hot. Gauging the temperature was therefore a matter of trial and error, even for the experienced ironer – no-one wanted scorch marks or burn-holes in their clothing. Box-irons were generally large and heavy, with a cavity underneath for a 'heater' (a slug of iron heated and then pushed into the cavity) that was kept in place by an iron slider. A box-iron was usually used with two heaters so one could be used while the other one was heating up on the fire. This type of iron was said to be much cleaner to use than the flat-iron, which came from the fire covered with soot and smuts and had to be cleaned off before use every single time. This was done by rubbing it across finely powdered bath-brick, something that was used in every English household. Bath-brick was not made from brick (although it was sold in brick-shaped blocks), but from 'a mixture of sand and clay deposited on the banks of the river Parret, at Bridgewater'.[26] This was then wiped off with a beeswax-impregnated cloth. A flat-iron was used with a linen cloth dipped in cold water which would catch any stray specks of soot or dirt. It was placed on a stand (perhaps a simple iron ring) or a trivet between uses.

Flat-irons were available in a range of weights from two to eight pounds, with the heavier models used for pressing very thick fabrics such as tweed. Because they were heated up on an open fire by being set upright against the bars of the grate, they were used with a holder made from thick layers of flannel to protect the ironer's hands from the intense heat. A popular way to test that a flat iron was ready to use was either to spit on the sole plate (the spit would sizzle and disperse) or, using a more genteel approach, dip a finger into water and dab it carefully on the sole plate. Flat-irons were also known as sad irons: the word 'sad' having the historical meaning of 'heavy', which is also the meaning of the French word *sourd*. The irons were prone to rust if left unused for some time, and had to be rubbed along the sole plate while still warm with a wax candle: this provided a moisture-proof barrier.

Italian irons (also known as tally or Dalli irons) were used for ironing frills, any item requiring a 'puffed' appearance, or velvet. An Italian iron consisted of a hollow tube on a swan-necked stand. A rod made of polished steel and with a wooden

26 *Dictionary of Daily Wants* 1861 p.106.

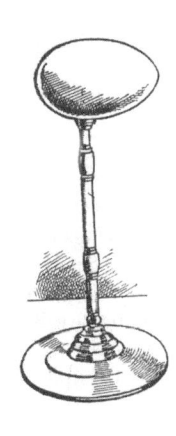

An egg iron for ironing the tops of sleeves (from *The Art and Practice of Laundry Work* p.55)

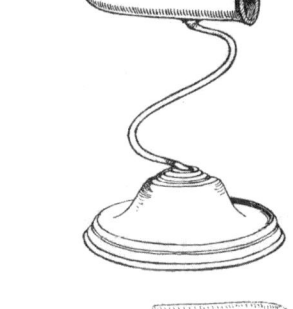

An Italian iron from around 1900 (from *The Art and Practice of Laundry Work* p.59)

Using goffering tongs (from *Practical Laundry Work* p.61)

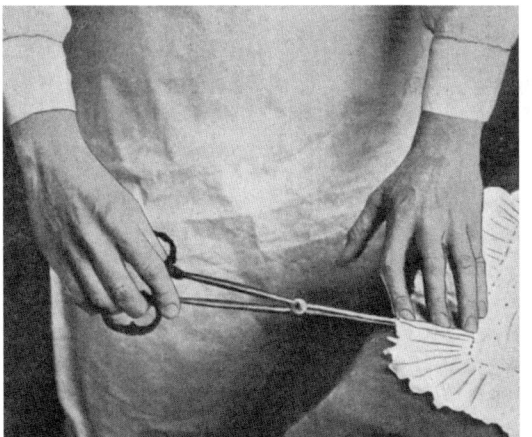

Ironing frills using the heel of the flat-iron (from *Practical Laundry Work* p.62)

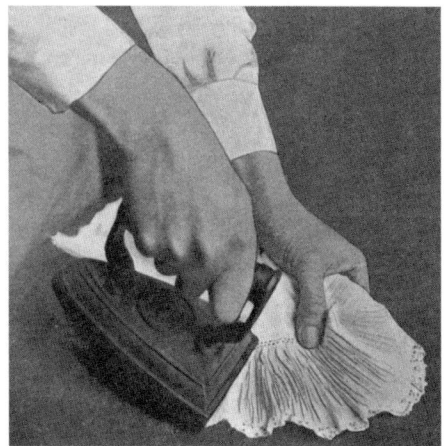

handle was heated and inserted into the tube and the items to be ironed were drawn across the heated tube. However, by the 1910s Italian irons were said to be out of favour and the new way to set frills was with a small amount of starching and a set of goffering tongs, a pair of which cost around 1s 6d. The word goffering was probably derived from the French word *gaufrer*, which means to crinkle. Goffering machines (turned by a handle) and goffering stacks (the material was threaded between thin slats held between vertical bars) were alternative ways of introducing a fashionable crimp or crinkled effect.

Ironing-stoves, also known as pagoda stoves because of their shape, were often used when there was a lot of ironing: lit initially with wood and coal, they had to be kept stoked with coke, which provided a good heat and was smut-free. A smaller type of ironing-stove, made of iron (which must have been extremely hot if anyone got too close to it) had the fire contained in a small box.

By the 1910s a few labour-saving innovations were creeping into wash-day, including a flat-iron shield that cost 1s. The patented Slip-On shield or 'slipper' fitted different-sized irons and had a nickel-plated surface that produced a good gloss without marking the clothes. The iron could therefore be heated over the fire and applied immediately to the clothes without the need for cleaning the plate – clearly a useful time-saver. The 'slipper' was still in use in the 1930s in houses that did not have gas or electricity. A high gloss was also obtained by

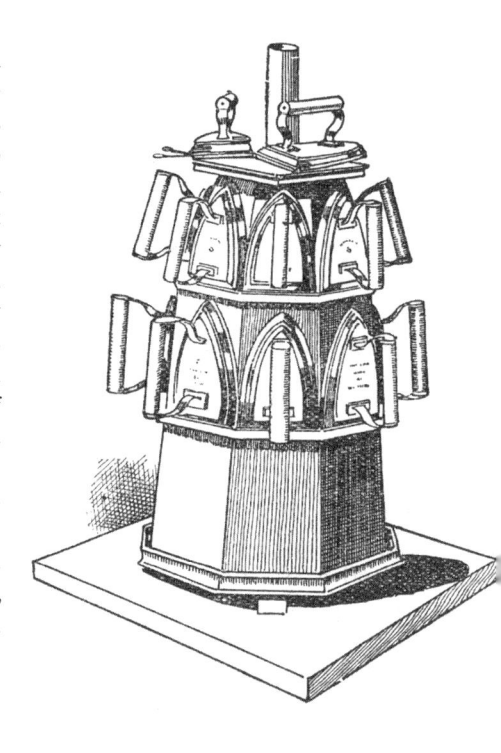

An ironing stove, circa 1900, for keeping flat-irons hot (from *The Art and Practice of Laundry Work* p.52)

An early electric iron from 1909: it would be plugged into a light socket (from *The Book of the Home* vol. 3 p.148)

27 Brown and Harris 2001 p.27.

a polishing iron, which had an oval rounded base made from polished steel, to polish cuffs or collars. By the beginning of the twentieth century irons that were heated by gas, methylated spirits or electricity were on sale, but many housewives continued to use those irons to which they were accustomed, often because there was no gas or electricity in their homes.

The major advantage of the new irons was the ability to control their temperature, and of course their cleanliness – no need for constant wiping with brick-dust and cloth. Gas irons in the 1930s contained interior gas jets that connected via a flexible pipe and bayonet connector to the nearest gas supply and were regulated by a small tap. A week's worth of ironing could be done in two hours for about ½d worth of gas. Gas had been used in the home since the nineteenth century and many homes were still lit by gas well into the twentieth century. The adoption of electricity, on the other hand, was very slow, partly because it took a long time to organise the many separate companies and local authorities into a cohesive whole and partly because many householders were nervous about using a current they couldn't actually see. As social historians Mike Brown and Carol Harris have pointed out, only about two percent of houses were wired up by 1910,[27] and it wasn't until the National Grid was set up in 1926 that new houses began to be routinely wired for electricity. By 1939 about three quarters of the houses in the UK were hooked up. The Electrical Association for Women, founded in 1924 with Caroline Haslett as its first director, was instrumental in encouraging women to see the labour-saving advantages of electricity and to get involved with the design of new products.[28] But the modern and the old-fashioned continued to operate side-by-side: even as late as the 1930s *The Concise Household Encyclopaedia* was still talking about ironing 'slippers' and bath-brick.

Advice books were very clear about the need for safety and common sense around electrical appliances, as electricity was still new in the domestic sphere. Electric irons at this time weighed between six and seven pounds, so a session at the ironing board was roughly equivalent to a decent modern workout with weights. Many older people will still recall the satisfyingly solid thump that followed each pass of the iron over the clothes in the years before lightweight models were available, not to mention the unique smell of just-ironed washing before the advent of fabric conditioners and man-made fibres such as polyester.

FROM FEATHER BOAS TO CORSETS

Fabrics such as cotton-polyester and viscose were unknown to our Victorian forebears, who wore serge, drill and holland (a linen fabric), as well as cotton and silk. Each strange and exotic fabric demanded a different treatment. In the early years of the twentieth century, many households sent unusual materials, such as feathers, skins, fur and silk, to the steam laundries, which also dealt with the cleaning of corsets, sunshades, sponges and hairbrushes.

Corsets were dipped in soapy water then straightened out on a board and brushed with a soft brush, dipping occasionally into water to loosen dirt. After rinsing and dipping them into hot-water starch to stiffen them, they were dried in the fresh air, then pressed to soften and smoothe them slightly. Cheap

28 Benjamin 1936 p.47;
www.engineeringtimelines.com

corsets were not easy to wash because the low-quality metal stays, once brought into contact with water, would rust.

Feather boas were squeezed between the hands in warm soapy water, rinsed, then squeezed again to remove the moisture (this was clearly not the time to use the mangle) and rolled in a cloth. The ends of the boa were then twisted and tied to a line, being shaken now and then to separate and fluff out the fronds. When dry, it was ready to be recurled. This was done by drawing a warmed blunt knife up through the fronds, curving them around the hand.[29] A survey of married working women before the Great War stated that feather-curlers working in factories were paid 1d to 2d per feather.[30]

Hairbrushes were swished up and down in a solution of soda and water, immersing just the bristles because soda would discolour the handle, often made of ivory. The brush was rinsed in cold water to stiffen the bristles.

Silk was dry-cleaned, which simply meant using a substance other than water. Petrol was much used as it did not 'alter appreciably the natural appearance of any fabric'.[31] It was, however, dangerous (not to mention the fumes and smell) and had to be handled with care. To dry-clean three silk blouses took a gallon of petrol mixed with two ounces of dry-cleaning soap: the garments were immersed one at a time and gently squeezed until clean. They were then rinsed in fresh petrol, squeezed lightly, rolled in a cloth and slapped hard to remove the moisture. The fumes evaporated while the garment was hung up to dry. Any ironing had to be done with great care as the heat of the iron could ignite both garment and worker too.

Skins such as grebe, with the feathers attached (perhaps on ladies' hats, which were often decorated with feathers in the 1910s), were washed in soapy water by holding the skin against the side of the tub and gently pouring cupped handfuls of

---

29 Rankin p.161.
30 Black 1913 (reprint 1983) p.44.
31 Rankin p.169.

A laundry-room in an upper-class home in the 1910s, with state-of-the-art machinery and a gulley set into the stone floor to allow the room to be hosed down (from *The Ideal Home* opposite p.266)

water down the length, pressing until the dirt was removed. Then it was placed on a cloth, pressed gently with the hand and hung in a dry place ready for remaking (easing it gently back into its original shape).

Sponges were washed in soda or, if they got too slimy, in a hot-water ammonia solution. A 1920s advice book suggested that making a knitted jacket for a bath-sponge would prolong its life by six years (bath sponges then were made from natural sponge rather than the synthetic varieties available today).[32] It's a sobering thought that housewives were encouraged to extend the life of their bath sponges this way. Nowadays we would just go out and buy another one – and would never contemplate keeping one for as long as six years – but when money was tight, as it was for so many in the post-Great War years, the female mind probably turned automatically to thrift. The book containing this novel idea (which is subtitled, with huge understatement, 'An effort to meet a need in the cheapest form') also suggested that starch could be made from the water used to boil potatoes or rice and that grated potatoes were good for cleaning cloth gaiters. The reader can made up their own mind as to whether the potatoes were eaten after this. Waste not, want not...

Sunshades and parasols were brushed inside and out with soapy water and a nail-brush, then water was poured over and a little gum-water applied. It was possible for this job to be done at home, but people who could afford to have a sunshade cleaned preferred to send it to a laundry, as the silk was often very fragile. Florence Jack, in *The Woman's Book*, put the price of an umbrella or sunshade at between 10s and 15s with a leather or waterproof canvas case costing upwards of 3s 4d.[33] However, according to social campaigner Clementina Black, the women who made such luxury items were paid extremely low

[32] *You & I Cookery Book* p.80.
[33] Jack 1911 pp.321-323

rates for their work, not helped by the fact that each process, from machining the covers, attaching the silk carrying rings and making the elastic bands that secured the covers, were all done by different women working from home. Elastic band cover-makers, for example, were paid 8d a gross (144) and makers of upmarket top-of-the-range sunshades had to buy a wide variety of sewing cottons in shades they might only ever use once.[34]

Swan's down was often used to trim middle-class children's coats and hoods, but was very fragile and clearly completely unsuited for its purpose because it quickly became matted and dirty. It was, however, easy to clean as it was simply swished gently in soapy water, rinsed and pressed dry, shaken up to separate the strands, and hung up near the fire.

The mysterious term 'flannels' appears to refer to the undergarments also known as 'combinations' that were everyday wear in the nineteenth to early twentieth century. There are accounts of Victorian children being literally sewn into their combinations over the winter, and people brought up in the 1950s may remember the final death throes of combinations in the vests that were known as liberty bodices, or in underwear made by Ladybird. Flannels (made usually either of knitted or crocheted wool, woven or made from flannel itself) were difficult to wash, as they would 'felt' and go hard if the water was too hot, and shrink if not washed and dried quickly enough. After an initial shake out of doors to remove dust, they were washed in lukewarm soapy water using soap jelly, squeezed and kneaded to remove dirt, rinsed in several lots of warm water, wrung out tightly using a wringer, shaken well and hung out to dry. Jaeger brand garments, which were popular round the turn of the twentieth century, were made of very thin wool and needed special care.

34 Black 1913 (reprint 1983) p.61.

They were steeped in a bowl of warm soapy water containing ammonia, covered to prevent evaporation of the ammonia, and left for 15 minutes before being washed in the normal way. One book explained that ammonia was an alkali that rendered grease and perspiration soluble and easy to remove in water – today, with a myriad of detergents at our disposal, we would simply use a pre-wash cycle and soap powder.[35] Flannels were also available in lighter fabrics such as delaine and nuns-veiling and, after washing, these were ironed inside out with a cool iron and stiffened slightly with gum-water. This was often used on delicate fabrics needing a little body (it's difficult to avoid such a pun as this is an accurate term), and was made by mixing two ounces of gum arabic with a pint of boiling water, then straining it through muslin. It was then bottled ready for use.[36]

Washing and 'getting up' lace, whether curtains or clothing, was a particularly fiddly business. If the lace was machine-made, also known as common lace, the laundress would steep it in cold water and then wash it in hot soapy water, taking care not to break the threads. White lace, especially if used for ladies' caps (many mature ladies wore lace caps indoors at the beginning of the twentieth century) often arrived at the laundry with yellow stains caused by the hair's natural oils – women generally had very long hair at this period and did not always wash it very often. The stains were removed by rubbing them with soap, rinsing in cold water, squeezing the water out and putting the lace in the sun to bleach naturally. The next step was starching, just enough to add a slight stiffness before ironing. A 'good, heavy iron'[37] pressed down well over a thick blanket-padded ironing sheet would bring the pattern up, and the job was done.

Real lace was handled with some care. If it was particularly

---

35 Humphry 1909 p.158.
36 Humphry 1909 p.150.
37 Rankin p.135.

old or fragile, it was tacked to a piece of old flannel before washing. Another way was to shake it gently in warm soapy water or swish it up and down in a wide-necked bottle of soapy water, then rinse it. Starch was not routinely used, but glycerine or sugar would stiffen it slightly. If the lace was white, it was dipped twice in a gum-arabic solution that contained a touch of blue (a blue dye available in small bags or as a loose powder, used as an optical brightener), squeezed, rolled in a cloth briefly and then pinned out, wrong side up, along the edge of the ironing-table. The next step required a lot of patience, as every 'point' and picot had to be pulled carefully into shape and pinned individually; every space had to be individually separated and blocked out until it was perfectly square and symmetrical. The lace was pinned along its width and left until almost dry, before ironing with a warm iron. A lace handkerchief would be treated in the same way – the muslin centre pinned into shape, the points and picots of the lace pulled out and pinned individually, and the lace left until almost dry. It is very likely that few housewives had time or inclination for such fiddly work and preferred to send their lace items to a careful laundry to be hand-finished.

Lace was often tinted to renew its colour prior to stiffening. Ecru (a shade between beige and cream) was popular, perhaps because it showed the dirt less than white. Ecru-tinted starch was available but was 'a very ugly colour'[38] so it was mixed with white starch until the desired shade was reached. Alternatively, tea-dyeing was less messy. This was done in much the same way as it is today (using leaf tea, as teabags hadn't been invented) except that a pinch of saffron was added to the little muslin bag of tea leaves, which was squeezed gently until the desired shade appeared. Tea leaves were often sold by enterprising cooks to dealers who knocked on kitchen doors,

38 Rankin p.136.

so there may have been occasions when housewives preferred to hang onto their spent leaves so they could use them for tinting purposes. Coffee essence (the brand known as Camp coffee was popular in the late nineteenth and early twentieth century) gave a darker cream colour or, if the fashionable string colour was required, the lace was dipped in an infusion of hay. Black lace was refreshed by dipping it in dark blue gum-water or in a mixture of milk and water if the lace needed stiffening. Ironing it through paper prevented an unsightly gloss.

One final technique, applied to Irish lace, was lace punching. Although this may conjure up all sorts of unlikely pugilistic images, the reality was simply that a small implement known as a lace punch or poker was applied to the back of Irish lace to bring the elaborate designs of flowers and trefoils into relief.

SECRETS OF THE LINEN CUPBOARD

When the bed or table linen and the family's clothes were washed, ironed, dried and folded, they were stored in a linen or airing cupboard. Large houses had a dedicated linen room fitted with slatted shelves. The linen cupboard in the average Victorian and Edwardian middle- or upper-class home would have been much like our modern equivalent, except for the quantities it contained: huge stacks of table and bed linen, divided into separate piles to indicate whether they were for general house use, for guests, servants or children. Items stored would have included dressing table mats, tray-cloths, bath towels and out-of-season curtains and blankets. *The Woman's Book* (published 1911) featured a sample list supplied by Waring & Gillow, a large London store, of 52 different items. In all, there were 500 pieces listed, costing more than £175.[39] This was a considerable sum of money and the list was clearly for a

39 Jack 1911 p.270.

large household (it recommended having more than six dozen table napkins), with social obligations (lots of tablecloths and bed linen) and with numerous servants (butlers' aprons and plenty of cloths for drying glasses).

The Victorian tradition of buying several dozen yards of linen at a time and then passing it down through the female side of the family meant that prosperous households stockpiled vast quantities and women were constantly on the lookout for further bargains at draper's sales. This squirreling urge vanished in the years after the Great War, as people began to move house more freely and also to move into smaller houses with less cupboard space. Women now began to select their linen more carefully, buying or making what they needed for immediate use rather than acquiring things they might never need. And, as new fabrics came onto the market, the old-fashioned linens and damask began to be seen as belonging to less enlightened, dowdier times and were often downgraded to use as polishing cloths or cut down for tray-cloths. The cult of the 'bottom drawer' or 'hope chest' still persisted as women engaged to be married collected and embroidered linen and pretty underclothes for use in married life: transfer patterns and needlecraft magazines provided lots of inspiration.

The 1911 linen list had included some extraordinarily large individual items. For example, a particularly splendid double damask tablecloth, clearly a 'best' tablecloth costing five guineas, was 18 feet long; standard tablecloths for the servants' hall measured 2 x 2½ yards; and linen hemstitched sheets, costing 42s, were over nine feet long. No wonder this photo shows two people folding a newly laundered tablecloth – it would have been impossible for one person to fold 18 feet of damp, lightly starched, heavy damask on her own. The way to do it properly was for two people to fold the cloth in half, take

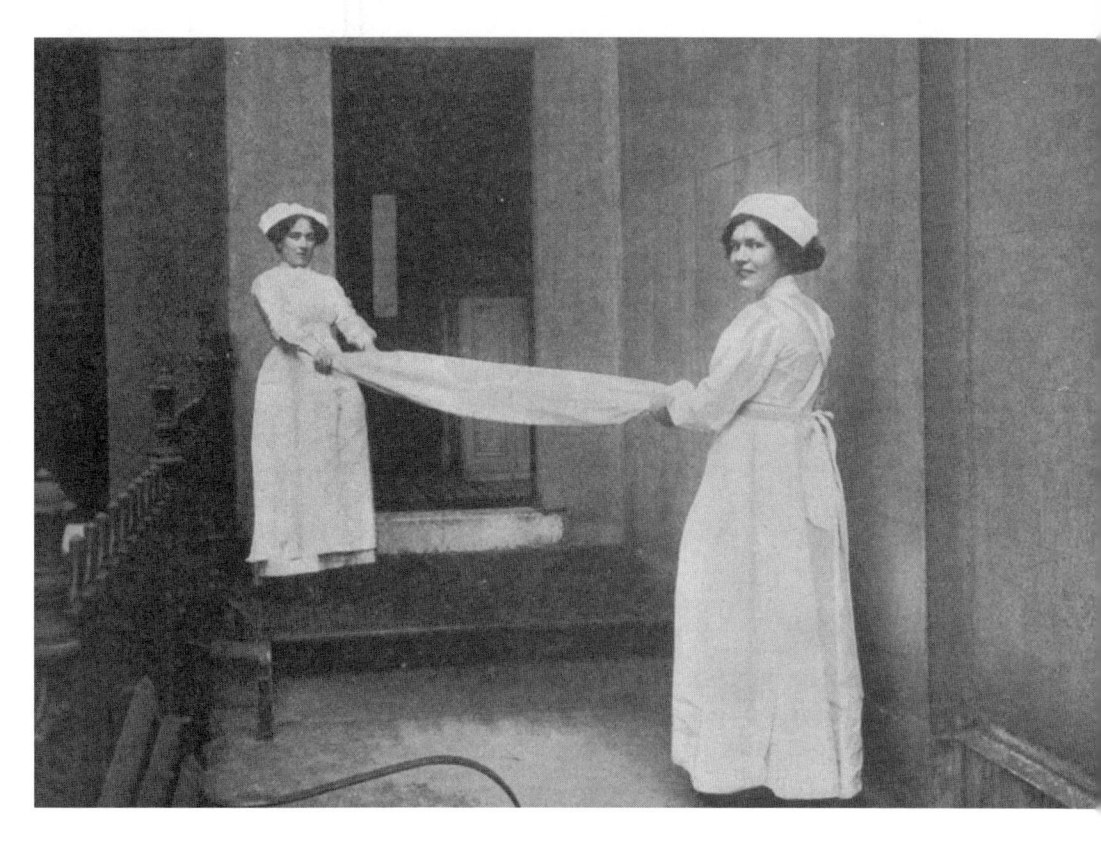

Edwardian servants demonstrate the correct way to fold large items (from *The Ideal Home* p.267)

it by its hemmed sides and shake it well; fold these sides together and, backing away from each other, draw the cloth out well; fold, back away and draw out twice more (cloth now in four folds); and finally turn the outside fold back so it met the centre fold, thus making one fold in the middle and two reverse folds either side equidistant from the centre.

THE PUBLIC WASHHOUSE: 100 GALLONS OF WATER ON TAP

Although some women ran small mangling businesses from home, washing machines and mangles were way beyond the financial reach of those urban working-class women living in small houses who could have got most benefit from them. However, new developments in public health and sanitation, plus an 1846 Act of Parliament that allowed local authorities to build public baths and washhouses, meant that households with access to a public washhouse (mainly in London and the industrial north of England) could take advantage of a range of facilities that they probably would otherwise never have afforded – much as people without washing machines do today with launderettes and washeterias.

The benefits included:

- no washing hung about to dry at home ("The small house is not rendered distasteful to husband and children by a steamy atmosphere, wet floors, and clothes hanging about")[40]
- plenty of working space, with hot and cold water
- the women were free to use as many coppers, tubs and mangles as they needed
- drying facilities (hot air cupboards)
- low cost – about 1½d per hour in 1895.

These innovations must have transformed the lives of the women who used them. One account stated that each woman had access to 100 gallons of water for washing the family's clothes: obviously no-one would have used this amount of water if they had to fill buckets, haul them to the tub and then heat it all up, even assuming that clean water was readily

40 Newsholme & Scott 1895 p.221.

available. It was therefore made easier for women to keep the family's clothes clean by paying regular visits to a washhouse (and indirectly to appreciate those twin joys so beloved of Victorian morality, cleanliness and godliness). A journalist, whose account was included in the 1902 compilation *Edwardian London*, observed that not only were there public washhouses in Shoreditch, Bermondsey, Westminster, Soho, Marylebone Street and Hackney but that there appeared to be a strict hierarchy of users. As most women preferred to get the washing out of the way as soon as possible, the most organised, tidy and 'respectable' housewives turned up in the early part of the week and the more dishevelled (and therefore, according to the value judgements of the time, the less respectable) followed later in the week.[41]

Public washhouses were designed with a lot of care and attention to detail. In the most modern examples (late 1890s) the floor was divided into self-contained stalls, each one fitted out with a rubbing board (A in diagram), a washing trough (B), a drainer (C), and a boiling trough (D). Linking each set of stalls and also separating them from each other were sets of drying horses (E) that ran on a rail and could be pushed in or out.[42] Each woman could therefore keep an eye on her washing from start to finish, so there could be no accusations of pilfering. It was also likely that the washhouses served a parallel function, that of a handy place for sociability or the passing on of gossip: the diagram in Newsholme & Scott shows that conversation could be carried on through the grilles around the compartments or, if the washer wished to 'keep herself to herself,' she could do her work in private.

Arthur Newsholme, co-author of *Domestic Economy: Comprising the laws of health in their application to home life and work* (1895) and Medical Officer of Health for

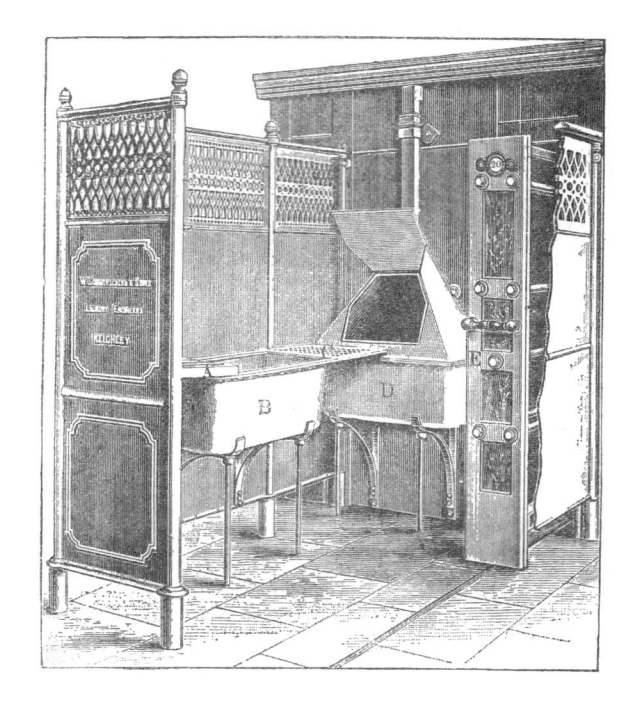

For women who did not have facilities at home, the public washhouse was cheap and convenient: this illustration shows a washhouse in the 1890s (from Domestic Economy *p.222)*

Brighton, pointed out that there was no danger of spreading infectious diseases in a public washhouse as all such diseases had to be reported to the area's sanitary officials, who were responsible for disinfecting any materials suspected of carrying disease.

THE COMMERCIAL LAUNDRY: A HOTBED OF VICE AND GOSSIP

By the beginning of the twentieth century many people had become reluctant to send their washing to a commercial laundry. They believed that the harsh chemicals ruined the

41 Sims 1902 (reprint 1990) pp.195-197.

42 Newsholme & Scott 1895 pp.222-223.

clothes; that 'other people's' washing might pass on germs; that the laundry women paraded around in the clothes they were supposed to be washing; that the practice of marking linen (essential so the workers knew which clothes belonged to which address) disfigured it; and that the machines were too hard on the clothes. Domestic machines were not much gentler, but there was said to be less wear-and-tear on clothes washed at home – and at least there was the chance of drying them in the fresh air. Also there were fewer chemicals used, and though there were germs, at least they were familiar ones. Households probably compromised by sending large articles such as sheets and towels to the laundry and doing the rest at home: this was by far the best practice in households with little space to spare for all the paraphernalia associated with washing and ironing.

There was another reason for the reluctance to send the washing 'out': laundries were thought to be poor at administration. Items were counted out and not counted back in, they returned clothes to the wrong people, and there were problems with unintelligible bills. Nevertheless, the printed forms that were available show not only the range of household washing dealt with by commercial laundries, but also the wide range of fabrics and finishes needing specialised care.[43]

Commercial laundries occupied an uneasy place in late-Victorian public consciousness. On the one hand they washed dirty clothing and 'got up' linen with often impeccable professionalism, but on the other they were seen as hot-beds of vice and immorality, full of gossip and bad language. Because of all this they were considered particularly unsuitable workplaces for young girls straight from school. Those linked ideals of cleanliness and godliness were stretched wide apart when it came to laundries: on top of the alleged vice and depravity was the fear that it would all 'rub off' on young

43 Miles p.73.

workers and morally pollute their young minds – and some girls were very young indeed. Fourteen was the minimum age for girls to start training as laundry maids, not because of worries about cutting short their education, but because they were thought not to be physically strong enough until they were fourteen. Training lasted for four years, after which a girl could apply for a job in a commercial laundry or, the dream job for many young laundresses, a post in a gentleman's laundry (the laundry attached to a large private house) and perhaps earn between £16 and £20 per year in the late 1880s.[44]

Work in a commercial laundry was extremely arduous, demanding a robust physique and strong arms, plus an ability to work long hours in a hot, steamy and often pressurised environment. There were reports that employers kept girls at work way past their allotted hours to deal with rush jobs from big concerns such as hotels.[45] Machinery used in Victorian laundries included powered wringers, hydro-extractors, boiling coppers and gas-heated ironing machines, and were belt-driven or gas fuelled, offering scope for injury from snapped belts or inhalation of fumes. According to trades union historian Barbara Drake, laundry workers were not included in the terms of the Factories and Workshops Act until 1895, following a lot of public demonstration. By the time the 1907 Act came in, however, there was provision for fans, ventilation and drainage as well as a limitation on the maximum hours that could be worked in a week to 68 including meal-breaks.[46] This indicates that perhaps women workers in this field could count on at least some protection from the sharp practice of their employers.

Almost inevitably, laundry work was seen as more than just a way of earning a living: by the early twentieth century it had acquired overtones of morality that had very little to do with

44 Mercier (ed.) 1885 p.142.
45 Mappen 1985 p.81.
46 Drake 1920 (reprint 1984) p.27; Wilson 1915 pp.340-341.

Smartly dressed 'finery ironers' at an Edwardian commercial laundry, using gas irons (from *The Book of the Home* vol. 3 opposite p.148)

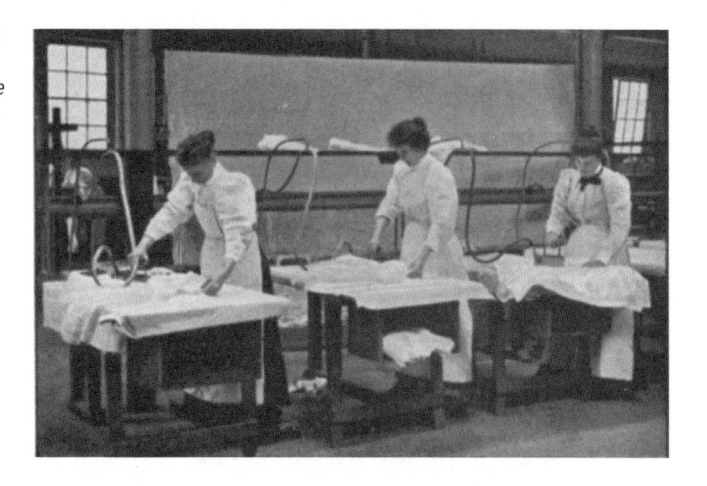

the job of getting dirty clothes clean. A good laundress was obedient (she had to learn the correct procedures and use them at all times or the consequences could be dire), industrious, neat-fingered, patient and good with routine. The Victorian preoccupation with respectability and self-help lingered into the twentieth century with an attitude not far removed from workhouse thinking: 'The main object of this work [i.e. this book] is to advance the cause of cleanliness, daintiness, and self-respect', said Louise Wetenhall in her preface to *Practical Laundry Work for Home and School*.[47] In other words, laundry work had become a respectable occupation and an appropriate vehicle for what might be termed do-gooding.

The Co-operative Society may well have contributed to this new attitude, as it was much concerned with choosing workers who would not bring the Society into disrepute. Already popular and with a wide customer base, the Co-op operated

47 Wetenhall, preface p.v.

There is no true white without blue', stresses this 1930s advertisement for Reckitt's Blue (from *The Home Book* p.141)

WHITE *is made of* SEVEN COLOURS!

Floating, shimmering soap-bubbles split up white light into seven colours. The colours of the rainbow that you see in the bubble are the colours that make pure white. One of these colours is blue. *There's no true white without blue.* White linens which have gone a yellowish-grey need blue to bring back their sparkling white. If you want your white things to come off the line as white as snow, remember to rinse them in Reckitt's Blue.

Reckitt's BLUE
Out of the blue comes the whitest wash!

laundries and also branched out in some areas into the associated trades of carpet-beating, dyeing and dry-cleaning.[48]

Small laundries were, of course, unable to compete with this level of versatility, and Margaret MacDonald, reporting for the Women's Industrial Council on a visit to a trade exhibition in 1907, observed that many small hand-laundries would soon be swallowed up by the larger firms who were so much more able to install powerful new machines and offer more services than their smaller rivals. However, she also pointed out that people who preferred a personal service would continue to patronise the smaller firms simply because the quality of the work that was done entirely by hand was far superior to that done in the commercial laundries. The trick was, and still is, to offer a niche market: in 1907 the niche market in the laundry trade dealt only with the most delicate and temperamental fabrics and the finishes that required the most skill and patience.[49] However, both commercial and small hand-laundries were to disappear with the increasing popularity of self-service launderettes and affordable domestic washing machines. Many well-known firms amalgamated or closed down, and many women lost their jobs as the task of getting the family's clothes clean returned to the domestic sphere. Laundries still survive but in far fewer numbers, with many of the survivors shifting their focus towards providing services for hotels and similar institutions. Most towns also have dry-cleaners where suits, duvets and other difficult-to-wash items can be cleaned, and self-service launderettes still flourish in many areas where accommodation is rented or is particularly compact.

Middle-class women were encouraged to enter the laundry trade but, inevitably, as managers rather than as 'hands'. According to *The Woman's Book* (1911) a three-month training course cost approximately 10 guineas inclusive of board and

[48] Wilson 1915 p.105.
[49] Mappen 1985 pp.70-71.

lodging, with several large London laundries offering training including The Wimbledon Laundry Co, in Cranbrook Road.[50] As well as a general aptitude for the work, laundry managers had to be good at administration and organisation, tactful when dealing with the complaining or fractious public, able to maintain discipline among the workers, and have a sound grasp of bookkeeping and commercial arithmetic. This is a very different (and much more useful) set of skills than that demanded of the working-class girls who were encouraged to enter the trade.

A TEXTBOOK APPROACH

The school subject known as Domestic Science was originally intended to instruct working-class Victorian girls in the basics of cooking, cleaning and washing. Poverty, over-burdened mothers, and inadequate or no cooking utensils often prevented girls from picking up all but the most rudimentary knowledge, and so schools began to introduce lessons in those areas of domestic life that were thought to be most useful for the girls' future, whether as a servant or a wife in her own home. Domestic Science was routinely taught to girls from the late nineteenth century until at least the 1970s, and was still being taught, both to boys and girls, in the late 1990s under the title Food Technology. The use of the terms 'science' and 'technology' seems to imply not only that the business of acquiring and cooking food had become distanced from the domestic sphere, but also that the 'science' aspect was somehow more important than the 'domestic'. It might be that this rebranding was intended to make cookery exciting and scientific to a generation raised in alienation from the business of food and cooking, but nowadays the focus appears to be too much on the science, and not enough on the practicalities.

50 Jack 1911 p.862.

At the end of the nineteenth century and the beginning of the twentieth, domestic science lessons for working-class schoolgirls would have included instruction in the art of laundry work. Today's teenagers would view the general tone of old textbooks with great derision, focussing as they did on the virtues of 'cleanliness, daintiness, and self-respect'.[51] It was clear that the whole, and only, point of the domestic science lessons was 'the fitting of women to be more efficient housekeepers'.[52]

Working-class girls were expected to be competent in a wide variety of housework-related jobs and to help their mothers from a very young age. This was partly because girls were expected to be able to cook, clean and keep house efficiently as a matter of course, and partly because there weren't enough hours in the day for the mother to do everything on her own – every household task took far longer than it does today because many houses had no running water, sanitation, heating or cooking facilities. Wages were low, rents were high and many houses were old and dilapidated, overcrowded and often crawling with bugs of various kinds. Under such adverse circumstances women needed all the help they could get, and put up heroic fights to keep their families clean, fed and clothed.

However, it is still somewhat difficult to appreciate the Victorian obsession with morality and cleanliness. It was seen as perfectly acceptable for writers of school textbooks, for example, to state that 'there is nothing more likely to aid in the development of character in children than the thorough inculcation of this science of cleanliness [i.e. laundry work]'. Teachers of the subject were instructed expressly to 'embrace the opportunity of instilling hygienic principles of cleanliness, and also influence the character of the pupils by the formation of habits such as punctuality, neatness, tidiness, carefulness, and

[51] Wetenhall preface p.v.
[52] Rankin p.9.

order'[53] – whether or not the household could afford to buy the necessary basic equipment, or indeed even had a water supply.

Although it is debatable how much girls actually learned and how far the teaching was relevant to their home circumstances, lessons in domestic laundry work were mapped out with almost military precision. Lessons for 12-year-olds in the 1910s were organised under the Five Step method outlined in detail by Margaret Cuthbert Rankin in *The Art and Practice of Laundry Work*:

- preparation (using prior knowledge to spark interest in a new subject)
- presentation (using 'reasoning and concentration' to understand the principles of the new subject)[54]
- association (linking relevant prior knowledge to the new subject)
- generalisation (bringing together all the newly acquired facts via question and answer, and writing it all up on the blackboard and in the pupils' notebooks)
- application (applying the principles learned).

The Five Steps were each subdivided into further steps called Demonstration, Observation and Suggestion, and Inference. Rankin's lesson notes cover more than 15 pages and include such gems as:

- *demonstration:* show the class a dirty zinc tub
- *observation and suggestion:* there is grease and dirt on the surface
- *inference:* zinc tubs become very greasy when used.[55]

53 Rankin p.9.
54 Rankin p.12.
55 Rankin p.13.

How long would modern teenagers put up with this sledgehammer approach to teaching? It is certainly thorough but must have been bewildering in the extreme for those girls whose mothers had no money for zinc tubs, no facilities and no water. It's a good bet that the average housewife, hurrying to get the washing finished so she could get onto the next job, would not have had time or inclination to pause and marvel at the fact of clean water becoming dirty, and dirty clothes becoming clean, but history is silent on this matter…

Before modern technology removed the slog from the daily grind, housewives had to proficient in a huge range of tasks. As this chapter shows, many women struggled with unwieldy heavy clothes, clumsy appliances and toxic chemicals in their own homes or worked long hours in hot steamy laundries washing other people's clothes, while belt-drives whizzed overhead, machinery rattled and fingers got crushed or burned. The one saving grace of laundry work was perhaps that the end-result – a pile of clean, dry, fresh and pressed linen and clothes – brought considerable satisfaction until, like housework, it all had to be done again the following week.

CHAPTER THREE

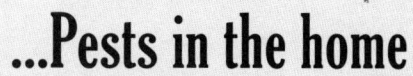

KILL IT...

...Pests in the home

Even the cleanest and most well-ordered homes had their problems, and writers of advice books were at pains to point out that a visitation of 'bugs' did not necessarily imply bad housekeeping or that abhorrent thing, a dirty house. In Victorian times, every kind of pest could thrive in the dark corners of oil-lit rooms and in the heavy draperies that were the prevailing fashion. Horse traffic, long skirts and ineffectual street-cleaning could bring the outdoors inside with unpleasant results. Flies, moths, fleas, bedbugs, lice, wasps, earwigs and mosquitoes were commonplace, and many houses also had mice, cockroaches, ants, and even crickets.

Battles with pests brought every household down to the same level. Cockroaches did not discriminate between rich and poor, or between clean and dirty houses: they simply took up residence, and it was then up to the human inhabitants to get rid of them. Fears were not confined to worries about hygiene: pests caused serious damage to pretty well anything they could get their jaws on. Some, such as ants and wasps, would invade sugar and jam; cockroaches ate shoe leather, whitewash and books; woodworm bored into furniture; moths destroyed woollen garments; rats ate almost everything; and silverfish would devour paper, glue, wallpaper and clothing.

Surveys of working-class life have described the fight to keep pests at bay, yet it was just as much a problem for the middle classes – a fact rarely acknowledged at the time. Jane Carlyle, diarist and wife of Thomas Carlyle, author of *The French Revolution: a History* (1837), was an exception: her diaries are peppered with complaints about pests and the methods she used to get rid of them.[1]

Today, we can just pick up an aerosol, handily labelled 'ant-killer' and spray it at the offending creature – our grandmothers

---

1 Holme 1965.

and great-grandmothers would have needed hands-on knowledge of a whole range of remedies and preparations. Our pest A-Z begins with some nineteenth-century remedies and their twentieth-century equivalents and ends with a look at our forebears' ideas on first aid for bites, stings and infestations. Don't be tempted to try these remedies yourself – some of the ingredients are dangerous to use. One of the worst substances was phosphorus, which was listed in a recipe for rat poison in the 1861 *Dictionary of Daily Wants* and was still being recommended in the 1910 edition of its successor, *Enquire Within Upon Everything*.[2] Handling phosphorus could result in the fatal condition known as phossy jaw, which infamously afflicted female workers in nineteenth-century match factories.

Sometimes new products were launched that did not turn out to be as safe as first thought: according to Rachel Carson's exposé of the pesticide business, *Silent Spring* (1962), the lethal DDT (dichloro-diphenyl-trichloro-ethane) was hailed in the 1930s as an efficient crop insecticide and was used in World War II to remove lice from refugees and soldiers. It was also, scarily, recommended for domestic use. A late 1940s edition of *Enquire Within Upon Everything* stated that in the home it was 'very generally used with excellent results' and recommended using DDT on bed bugs, fleas, ants, flies and mosquitoes.[3] By the 1950s DDT was being recommended for use on a wide range of domestic items from pantry shelves and light-fittings (to kill flies) to clothes and wardrobe interiors (to kill clothes-moths). Marguerite Dodd, author of *America's Homemaking Book* (1957/1968) recommended using DDT either in a spray-gun or aerosol, or as a spray attached to a vacuum cleaner, but did emphasise that it should be used with caution because of its toxic qualities.[4] One of the problems with DDT, as Carson made clear, was that it passed from

2 *Dictionary of Daily Wants* 1861 p.834; *Enquire Within* 1910 p.398.
3 *Enquire Within* 1910 p.133.
4 Dodd 1957 (reprint 1969) p.202.

Even as late as the 1950s, advice books were recommending DDT as 'the housewife's best weapon against moth and other pests', suggesting that a spray gun be used 'generously and often' (from *Newnes Home Management* p.447)

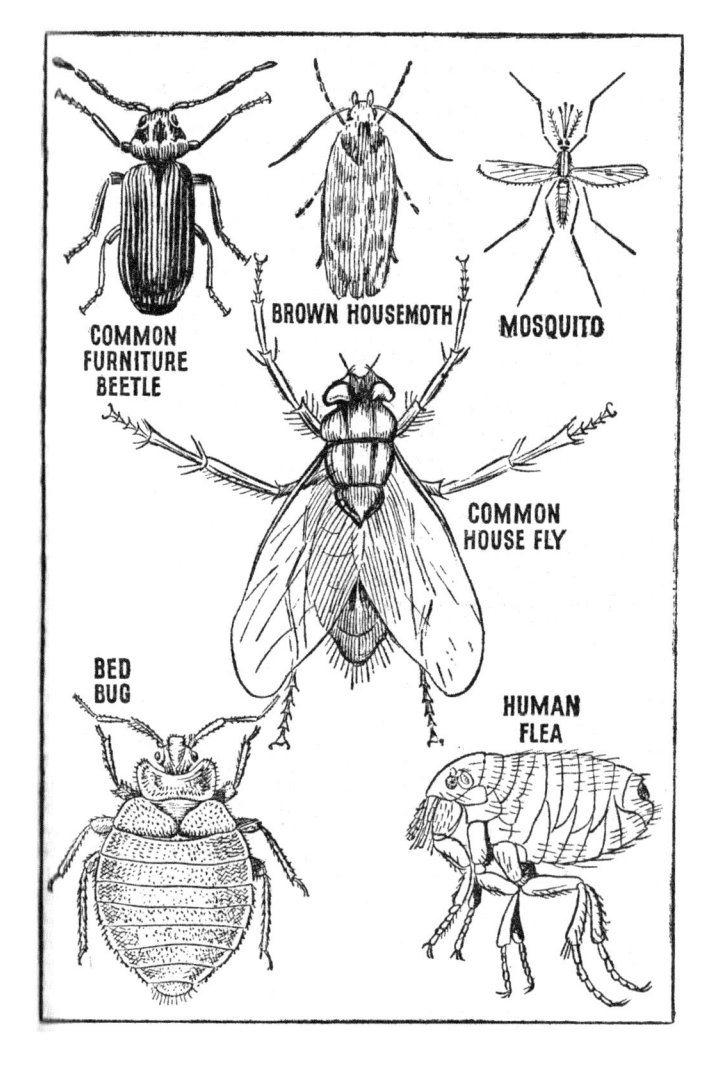

An identification chart of pests – cockroaches, woodworm, ants and silverfish are absent (from *The Book of Hints and Wrinkles* p.155)

The Demon Beetle Trap from 1909 (from *The Book of the Home* vol. 3 p.132)

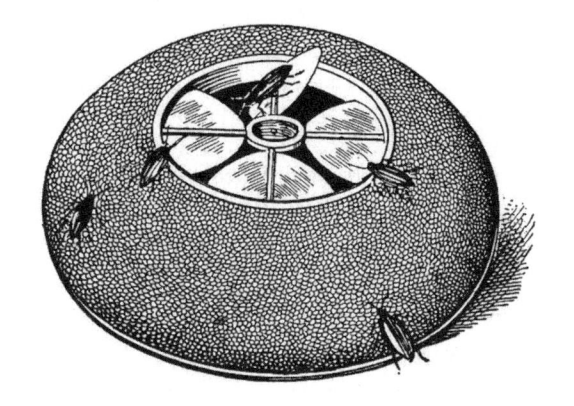

organism to organism: if crops were sprayed with DDT, the hens that were fed meal made from these crops laid eggs containing DDT. Humans were then eating DDT-contaminated eggs. DDT was banned in the UK in the 1970s.[5]

NINETEENTH-CENTURY REMEDIES

- *ants:* hang a small bag filled with camphor in food cupboards
- *bed bugs/bed ticks:* sprinkle oil of lavender between the sheets (said to be the best way of dealing with bedbugs while travelling)
- *beetles:* trap them using the 'Demon'
- *cockroaches:* hide away anything edible – including shoes. Cockroaches would eat the lot and import their friends and relations to join the feast
- *crickets:* stuff Scotch snuff into their exit holes
- *flies:* a mixture of quassia and moist sugar (quassia is a shrub, the bark of which was used as an insecticide; moist sugar may have been Demerera sugar or simply sugar moistened with water)

5 www.en.wikipedia.org

- *rats and mice:* a pound of hog's lard (fat from a pig's abdomen: melted down or 'rendered' it had many culinary and medicinal uses) mixed with an ounce of phosphorus and a pint of proof whisky, added to a mixture of flour, sugar and water, rolled into pellets, flavoured with oil of aniseed and laid in rat holes. The book added that this idea originated with a Doctor Ure – hopefully he did not sample his own recipe. The rats must have glowed in the dark as well as reeling about drunk from the whisky.[6]

TWENTIETH-CENTURY REMEDIES

By the 1930s living conditions had improved for some (but by no means for everyone). New fashions in interior decorating and furnishing demanded a sternly minimalist style that owed its look in part to the ideas connected with labour-saving that were at last beginning to reach the average housewife. New houses were smaller than their Victorian counterparts, with electricity 'laid on', were less likely to be infested with insects, and had fewer cupboards where surplus clothes, paper or junk might attract pests. Appliances such as vacuum cleaners, long-handled mops and electric polishers were easy to use and required no bending, kneeling or scrubbing: it was therefore so much easier to keep a house clean that by 1936 housewives were being warned against over-zealous cleaning and advised not to worry too much about the odd crumpled cushion or scattered crumb.[7] Advertisements told a different story: tiled floors polished to a glassy (and lethal) shine with Cardinal, fire surrounds gleaming with Zebo, kitchens smelling of San-pic pine disinfectant all hinted that the only way to a 'real' home was by constant and thorough cleaning.

Although pests attacked both rich and poor, some pests preferred to move into households with plenty of scope for

6 *Enquire Within* 1910 p.398.
7 Benjamin 1936 p.2.

Food kept in tins was protected from ants, silverfish and mice (from *The Book of the Home* vol. 2 p.26)

the operation of their skills. Houses with fitted carpets and upholstered furniture, or wardrobes containing furs or fur coats, were popular targets for moths and woodworm; untidy kitchens with shelves carelessly piled with paper bags and cardboard boxes were ideal accommodation for ants and flies. This is perhaps one reason why kitchen cabinets became so popular in the 20s and 30s: foodstuffs could be decanted into neat rows of matching containers with lids; flour could be emptied into a purpose-built flour-hopper rather than kept in its (pest-edible) paper bag; and everything could be stored neatly out of sight behind the cabinet's glass doors. Cabinets came in a variety of sizes and were ideal for small kitchens.

The Holborn rattrap (from *The Book of the Home* vol. 3 p.134)

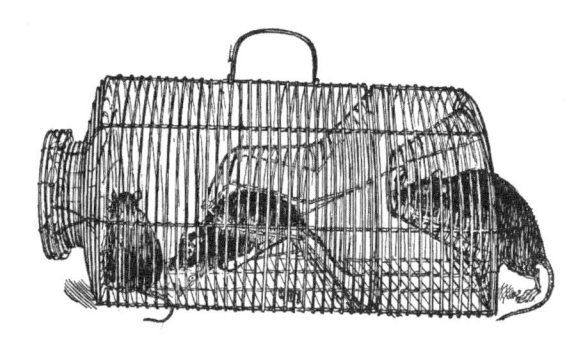

Many houses built at this time also had a larder with slate or marble shelves for the storage of perishables, or a stone slab where food could be kept cool (refrigerators were too expensive for the majority of households in the 1930s).

Rats were a particular and worrying problem, and despite the fact that in 1919 government legislation had been introduced in the form of the Rats and Mice (Destruction) Act, the existence of an Annual Rat Week showed that the pest problem persisted. Indeed, a Mr W.H. Green asked the Minister of Agriculture in 1938 whether one Rat Week per year was sufficient.[8] According to the Minister, Mr W.S. Morrison, a single annual concentration of destruction focussed the public's minds on the job in hand. He also pointed out that it was local authorities who were responsible for enforcing the Act throughout the year. Under its terms, occupiers of land or buildings were bound to take 'all appropriate steps' to destroy rats on their premises or risk a fine of £5 (1930s rates). Although the Protection of Animals Act of 1911 had restricted the use of poisons, it was defensible for anyone to say that they were using poisons in order to kill rats.[9] There was much discussion on this topic in Parliament in 1919, indicating that

8 www.google/national-rat-week
9 Hammerton (ed.) p.1046.

the rat problem was a serious one: Lord Lee of Fareham, (Hampshire), President of the Board of Agriculture and Fisheries, was instrumental in clarifying various obscure clauses of the Act so that the Local Authorities knew exactly what powers were at their disposal. This included suggesting that fines be increased from £5 to £20.[10]

By the 1930s more proprietary pest-killing products were available in shops such as the Army & Navy Stores, including Flypic, O-Cedar Fly Spray and the Era Moth Killing Cartridge and Wardrobe Sachet. At the same time, housekeeping manuals continued to offer traditional remedies based on chemicals sold by chemists or hardware shops.

- *ants:* drop quicklime into the nest and pour boiling water over. Wormwood (a bitter-tasting shrub) was said to drive away black ants while wintergreen (a plant with a pungent smell) or ground ivy would remove red ants. Another solution was to dig a trench across their path and fill it with paraffin
- *bed bugs:* with a small brush, rub 3d worth of spirits of naptha (a flammable oil) into the bedstead, mattress and springs. One bug poison included corrosive sublimate (bichloride of mercury – a poison)[11] and oil of turpentine. That a special fumigation kit was available in the 1930s indicates that bed bugs were still a problem despite advances in hygiene and housing: it consisted of formalin (a watery solution of formaldehyde – a poison) in a metal case and a small spirit burner for heating it up.[12] Another solution was to spray rooms with the wonderfully named Eradico, as recommended in a 1930s nursing textbook.[13] Pests such as bed bugs have not disappeared, despite energetic work by generations of housewives and pest

10 www.hansard.millbanksystems.com/lords/1919/nov/20/rats-and-mice-destruction-bill
11 Hammerton p.305.
12 *Book of Hints and Wrinkles* p.154.
13 Pugh 1936 p.52.

controllers. A recent search online brought up an article offering advice that would not have been out of place 100 years ago, including removing clutter from under the bed, keeping everything clean and washing bed linen at a high temperature[14]

- *cockroaches, beetles and blackbeetles:* bait a jam-jar with an inviting mixture of beer and bananas, attach small runways made of paper or wood and smear them with the bait. Fix a wide paper funnel to the top of the jar, and the cockroaches will pay but one visit.[15] Bugs could also be fumigated by burning sulphur or enticing them with cucumber skins which 'has the effect of stupefying them'.[16] One remedy labelled (with good reason) 'DEADLY POISON' comprised pyrethrum powder (an insecticide made from plants of the daisy family), snuff, cayenne pepper, white arsenic and corrosive sublimate.[17] Black beetles, which were neither black nor beetles, were 'believed to be directly connected with the transmission of the cancer virus' according to a 1930s invalid cookery book[18]
- *fleas:* sprinkle Persian powder over flea-infested bedding or just sprinkle salt in bedding – this remedy was said to be 'simply marvellous'[19]
- *flies:* swat them; leave saucers of cold green tea, well sweetened, around the room; or hang up flypapers smeared with tangle-foot mixture such as castor oil and powdered resin. Flies and their eggs on and around windowsills could be killed with a damp duster, the woodwork then washed over with Sanitas (a popular disinfectant) and water. Flies could be kept out of the house by putting a mesh screen in an open sash window, painting the kitchen woodwork blue (a popular folk

Mesh food covers protected against flies (from *The Book of Hints and Wrinkles* p.156)

14 Google search on 'bedbugs' Nov 2010.
15 Minter 1927 p.81.
16 Humphry 1909 p.132.
17 Minter 1927 p.132.
18 Meighn 1928 p.32.
19 Kirk p.309.

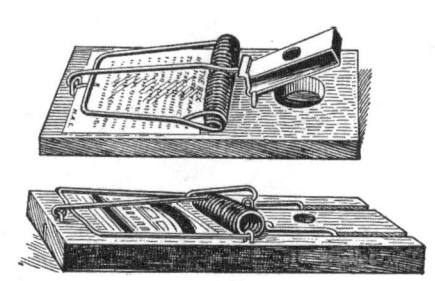

The Veto and Hero mousetraps
(from *The Book of the Home*
vol. 3 p.134)

remedy that often appeared in advice manuals), or hanging up a bunch of fresh nettles. To keep them from settling on milk (which was then usually kept in a cool place, either on the stone floor or on a marble shelf), squares of muslin were laid over the milk jugs and weighed down with beads at the four corners

- *mice and rats:* daub a rat with tar and set it loose so the unpleasant smell will disperse the rest of the colony (quite how you caught the rat in the first place or avoided a nasty bite while applying the tar was not explained). Or, to employ slightly more subtle rodent psychology, make a small island in the middle of a tub of water dug into the ground: the mice would fight for a place on the island rather than swim to safety, and all but the strongest would drown.[20] Mice and rats could be deterred by cutting off all sources of food, cleaning away any refuse, covering the dustbin, and filling up all holes with sand or broken glass. If none of this worked (and judging by the efforts made during Annual Rat Week, the problem was a major one) there was always poison (sold as paste to spread on cheese or strong-smelling food such as a kipper), bait (such as extract of red squill, a poisonous plant available in powder form from the chemist),[21] or simply keeping an energetic cat or small terrier as a rat-catcher. Traps were also used: gin traps, toothed spring traps, wire traps (a rectangular box with a spring) and varnish or birdlime traps (strong lithographic varnish spread on a sheet of cardboard)
- *silverfish:* poison them with pyrethrum powder, either on its own or combined with powdered borax and sodium fluoride. These pests ate anything made from paper and

20 Minter 1927 p.82.
21 Hammerton p.1048.

would swarm about in cupboards in search of crumbs
- *wasps:* direct the fumes from cyanide of potassium into the nest.

FIRST AID

Not only were houses infested with parasites and insects: people also cross-infected each other at school, on public transport and in shops and crowds, and could hardly go around dusted with pyrethrum powder or festooned with fly-papers. Some people today may remember regular visits by the 'nit nurse' to their school, or having steel combs wrenched through their hair in an attempt to comb out head-lice. Some of the home remedies offered for those afflicted with lice, fleas and other horrors were fairly grisly – and in some cases, fairly risky too.

- *mosquito bites:* wash with diluted iodine and then apply ammonia or a paste of bicarbonate of soda and sal volatile (most often used as smelling-salts: its pungent smell was good for reviving ladies from fainting fits)
- *fleas:* sprinkle underwear with peppermint essence or chloroform – this was a 1930s remedy that would not only advertise to everyone that you had fleas, but would emit a powerful smell at close quarters
- *head lice:* rub hair well with artificial oil of sassafras or crude paraffin, taking care to avoid naked flames afterwards.[22] Other remedies included applying powdered parsley seed to the roots of the hair, and rubbing a mixture of honey, sulphur, vinegar and sweet-oil onto the scalp (this was recommended for children with head lice)
- *body lice:* disinfect underclothes using steam and apply

Dealing with bites, strings, bumps and scratches was all in the daily round of housewife's skills (from *The Secret of Health and Comfort* p.52)

22 Pugh 1936 p.51.

A cupboard full of dodgy chemicals provided a solution to every pest-related ailment (from *The Secret of Health and Comfort* p.18)

stavesacre ointment (the stavesacre plant is mentioned in Culpeper's Complete Herbal),[23] iron any seams of infested clothing (the lice liked to get into seams), or, as soldiers in the Great War trenches were said to do, pick them out and squash them between the fingers

- *scabies (a contagious and very itchy skin disease caused by the itch mite):* soak affected parts in hot water and scrub with soft soap, then apply diluted sulphur ointment and follow up with calamine lotion (this was used to cool the effects of sunburn or itchy conditions such as measles)
- *internal parasites such as worms:* swallow one drachm (equivalent to one eighth of a fluid ounce) of oil of male fern followed, after a four-hour interval, by castor oil.[24] The male fern plant was a powerful remedy for tapeworm. Threadworms were treated by swallowing castor oil, or a mixture of calomel and santonin (calomel was a mercury-based toxic substance). Then the patient took a salt-water enema that had dilute mercurial ointment in it, to ease discomfort. As santonin apparently turned urine bright yellow, the patient would have had an interesting surprise.[25] Some of these remedies listed in nineteenth-century nursing textbooks were still being recommended in the 1930s.

Happily, some ailments had slightly less aggressive treatments: wasp stings in the throat or mouth were eased by chewing a raw onion (the taste of the onion was probably intended to mask the pain of the sting); gnat stings were eased by applying carbolic acid and vinegar; and stings in general were covered with a slice of raw onion or a dollop of garden soil (and a fervent hope to avoid lockjaw).[26]

23 Pugh 1936 p.52; Culpeper p.354.
24 Craig p.222.
25 Pugh 1936 p.53.
26 Kirk p.243.

People may still remember calamine lotion (sold in tubes or bottles) applied to the majority of insect bites and stings, or, even easier, cold milk or witch hazel dabbed on with cotton wool. Modern thinking on stings is much more specific than in the past, pointing out, for example, the dangers of anaphylactic shock and the need for immediate medical aid in such cases – chewing raw onions would hardly be countenanced today. We are also able to take advantage of a wide range of homeopathic, aromatherapy and 'alternative' remedies specially formulated for bites, stings and localised itches. Some of these remedies are themselves based on those used in the past by our grandmothers and great-grandmothers, who had to deal not only with bites, stings and pests but with accidents, illnesses and the bumps and scratches of everyday life as well – and all before the advent of micropore tape, penicillin and the National Health Service.

If you think life was tough for the British housewife, remember that British women of the Raj had a few additional, and more exotic, problems to worry about. Scorpions and snakes were common in India and women were expected to know how to deal with them efficiently and calmly. Steel and Gardiner, authors of the classic stiff-upper-lip guide for memsahibs, *The Complete Indian Housekeeper and Cook* (1893), included hints on treating scorpion- or snake-bites, as well as bites from mad or 'doubtful' dogs.[27] Clearly the memsahibs needed strong stomachs to carry out these cures. Scorpion-bites were covered with a paste made from ipecacuanha (a flowering plant used in medicine to induce vomiting or coughing); dog-bites were carved out as deeply as possible with a penknife and the resultant gaping, bleeding wound cauterised with nitrate of silver (silver nitrate is used nowadays to remove warts and verrucas), carbolic acid or hot

27 Steel and Gardiner 1893 p.195.

> **SNAKES**
> CRAWL ON THEIR OWN STOMACHS;
> **FLEAS**
> ARE NOT SO PARTICULAR.

Working-class, middle-class or upper-class homes, it was all the same to a flea (postcard circa 1910)

iron. A toe or finger that had been bitten by a snake was tied with a ligature or tight cord which was then twisted tighter with a stick. An amputation was performed if necessary and, if this could not be done, the flesh was cut right round the bone and the victim urged to suck the wound until it could be cauterised. The patient (probably already in shock from the initial bite and from the horror of the treatment) was then plied with brandy – and the memsahib probably needed a stiff drink herself. A mustard plaster was then placed over the patient's heart and their limbs were massaged. Mustard plasters were in common use in Britain too, according to *The Dictionary of*

Daily Wants (1861), providing relief for chest and abdominal pains in the interval before a professional arrived.[28] Fresh mustard was mixed with cold water just as it would be prepared for table use, spread on paper or a thin fabric such as calico, and applied to the skin for 20 to 30 minutes: this was apparently as long as most patients could stand. The remedy was still recommended for use in the 1930s: *The Concise Household Encyclopedia* claimed that it was 'a handy and reliable emetic'.

We should count ourselves fortunate that we're no longer called upon to amputate fingers, participate in Rat Week, replace wallpaper that's been chewed by silverfish, or to spray DDT on every surface in the home. However, perhaps we should spare a thought for the generations of women who kept their surroundings clean by constant work and vigilance, armed with little more than bunches of herbs, a strong shoe and a cupboard full of dodgy chemicals.[29]

28 *Dictionary of Daily Wants* 1861 pp.700-701.
29 Hammerton (ed.) p.830.

CONCLUSION

Anyone who has struggled to use and wash heavy cast-iron pans, picked bits of dried starch out of their fingernails, or scratched at mosquito or flea bites will find common cause with the heroic fight put up by our grandmothers and great-grandmothers who coped with all these and much worse, without the benefit of the NHS, health and safety regulations, or a whole slew of Public Health Acts. Probably no-one today would even think of making their own soap, sanitising metal dustbins by burning newspapers in them, or rubbing stings with garden soil, yet our forebears practised a remarkable brand of thinking-on-their-feet ingenuity in dealing with problems and crises, and with daily life in general.

In a world where there are off-the-shelf products to cope with every conceivable household task, and supermarkets open 24-hours-a-day in which to buy them, such home-grown skills have probably disappeared for good. Even in an era when many wives and mothers are probably holding down a full-time career as well as running much of the household, live-in domestic servants are a rarity. Au pairs or 'dailies' would hardly take kindly to starting work at 6.30am and being faced with the gargantuan lists of tasks regularly tackled by 14-year-olds in households in the early years of the twentieth century. The era of domestic advice books also appears to have passed, although recent TV shows like *How Clean Is Your House?* and *Wife Swap* offered an opportunity for some vicarious horror at other people's lack of domestic skills, and the US website flylady.net has attracted a huge following by advocating that women develop a cleaning routine that begins with polishing their kitchen sink every morning, writing these routines into something called 'My Control Journal'.

Old advice books are a unique source of information, giving us an insight into the expectations, aspirations and codes of conduct of the times. Trends in table linen, the advance of electricity across the country, the idea that phosphorus was an acceptable substance to use in the home – so much social history is bound up within the battered maroon, sage green or buff bindings of the early twentieth-century domestic advice book. Women were expected to marry, to raise children, to run their own homes and to be content with their lot. As historian Virginia Nicholson pointed out, this expectation was derailed by the plain fact that after the carnage of the Great War there were not enough men left alive for them to marry.[1] Advice books appear to have ignored this not inconsiderable problem (although a great deal of women's fiction over the next 30 years focused on the 'Surplus Woman' situation) and concentrated instead on the joys of domesticity and homemaking and the delights of parenthood. Advice books constantly reinforced the thinking that a woman's place was in the home by making cosy references to hubby and wifey and the kiddies, to 'wifedom as a serious life's career'[2] and the home as 'the pivot round which all her main interests revolve'.[3] Husbands appeared occasionally in advice-book photographs, pipes clenched firmly in teeth, doing manly things with tools or digging in an immaculate garden, and increasingly wives were pictured

1 Nicholson 2007.
2 Marshall (ed.) *Complete Illustrated Household Encyclopaedia*, p.v.
3 Marshalll (ed.) *News Chronicle Housewife's Handy Book* p.197.

holding the end of a roll of wallpaper or wielding a paintbrush. Married life between the wars was, in the world of advice books at least, less hierarchical than in the nineteenth century and more of a partnership of equals; indeed one popular image was that of husband and wife 'pulling loyally together' in the interests of the home.[4] However, women expected to work hard at learning housewifely skills and anyone who has become competent at the many jobs and routines that keep the average modern family home ticking over will appreciate that our grandmothers had a lot more responsibilities than we do today. They also had so many skills that are lost to us, including thrifty food shopping and ways to use up bits and pieces that we nowadays simply throw away. Our grandmothers may have been 'only housewives' but they were certainly experts at their job. Show any woman born before 1939 a dead rabbit, a basket of plums and a pail of dandelions and she will probably know exactly what to do with them to produce a decent meal, a pan of stock, a bottle of polish and a glass of wine.

---

[4] Marshall (ed.) *Complete Illustrated Household Encyclopaedia*, p.v.

GLOSSARY

Many of the weights, measures, currency and prices in this book belong to the pre-decimal era (before 1971) and need some explanation. People who grew up in pre-calculator days were drilled at school to do fiendish sums such as £3 16s 3d + 17s 6½d + 9 ¾d in their heads, but modern thinking prefers computers to mental arithmetic and the comfortable decimal to fiddly fractions.

CURRENCY

Before 1971, money was divided into pounds (written as £), shillings (written as s) and pence (written as d – short for denarius). There were 20 shillings in a pound and 12 pence / pennies in a shilling, making 240 pennies in a pound.

Whereas the smallest coin in modern money is 1p, our grandparents had a number of very small denomination coins such as sixpences, threepences, halfpennies (two to a penny) and farthings (four to a penny). Working upwards, there were florins (2s), half-crowns (2s 6d), half guineas (10s 6d), guineas (£1 1s) and sovereigns (originally a gold £1 coin). Banknotes started at 10s and a five-pound-note was not only a rare sight, but seemed as big as a tablecloth.

The value of money has also changed. £1 in modern money might have bought approximately £100-worth of goods during the time-span of this book, or, to use a different comparison, £1 in 1896 was worth approximately £7 6s in 1970.

WEIGHTS

Modern metric weights are very different to old imperial ones. We now buy in kilos and grams, whereas our forebears bought in stones, pounds and ounces:

- 1 ounce = 28.35g
- 1 pound (1lb) = 16 ounces / oz = 0.4536 kg
- 1 stone = 14lb = 6.35kg
- 1 lump of sugar refers to sugar that was compressed into small cubes: it's still available today in this form
- A pinch (of saffron, borax etc) is the amount pinched up between the thumb and forefinger

VOLUME

Pints and gallons are now measured in litres and millilitres, while some measures are used only in specialised professions such as pharmacy.

- 1 drachm = ⅛ a fluid ounce / ¹⁄₂₀ a pint / 0.028l
- 1 gill = ¼ pint / 5 fl oz
- 1 pint = 20 fl oz
- 1 quart = 2 pints / 1.3 l
- 1 gallon = 8 pints / 4.546 l

BIBLIOGRAPHY

BOOKS

'A member of the aristocracy', *Duties of Servants*. Frederick Warne, 1899.

Abell, L.G., *A Mother's Book of Traditional Household Skills*. Lyons Press, USA, 2001 (first published 1852).

Barnes, Alison (ed.), *Home Management* (vol.1). Newnes.

Bateman, R.A., *How to Own and Equip a House*. R.A. Bateman.

Beddoe, Deirdre, *Back to Home and Duty: Women Between the Wars 1919-1939*. Pandora, 1989.

Bell, Florence, Lady, *At the Works: a Study of a Manufacturing Town*. Virago, 1983 (first published 1907).

Benjamin, Thelma, *Everyday in my Home*. Ivor Nicholson & Watson, 1936.

Black, Clementina, *Married Women's Work*. Virago, 1983 (first published 1915).

Book of Hints and Wrinkles. Odhams.

Brown, Mike and Harris, Carol, *Wartime House: Home Life in Wartime Britain 1939-1945*. Sutton Publishing, 2001.

Carson, Rachel, *Silent Spring*. Penguin, 1991 (first published 1962).

Chesterton, Mrs Cecil, *I Lived in a Slum*. Gollancz, 1936.

Cottington-Taylor, Mrs D.D. (ed.), *Home Book*. Reckitt & Colman.

Craig, Elizabeth, *Elizabeth Craig's Household Library: Housekeeping*. Collins.

Culpeper, Nicholas, *Culpeper's Complete Herbal*. Foulsham, (first published 1653).

Davidson, Caroline, *Woman's Work is Never Done: a History of Housework in the British Isles 1650-1950*. Chatto & Windus, 1982.

Dictionary of Daily Wants. Houlston & Wright, 1861.

Drake, Barbara, *Women in Trade Unions*. Virago, 1984 (first published 1920).

Enquire Within upon Everything. Madgwick, Houlston and Co. Ltd, 1910 (106e).

Enquire Within upon Everything. Herbert Jenkins (122nd edn).

Every Woman's Book of Home-Making. Amalgamated Press.

Fairclough, M.A., *Lloyd's Practical Household Management*. Lloyd's Weekly News, 1913.

Good Housekeeping's Home Encyclopaedia. Caxton Publishing Co., 1967 (first published 1951).

Hammerton, J.A. (ed.), *Concise Household Encyclopedia*. Educational Book Co.

Hardyment, Christina, *From Mangle to Microwave: the Mechanisation of Household Work*. Polity Press, 1988.

Holme, Thea, *The Carlyles at Home*. Oxford University Press, 1979.

Home of To-Day. Daily Express.

Hooper, Mary, *Nelson's Home Comforts*. Nelson, Dale & Co., 1893 (14re).

Horn, Pamela, *Women in the 1920s*. Alan Sutton, 1995.

Humphry, Mrs C.E. ('Madge' of Truth), *Book of the Home*. Gresham Publishing Co., 1909.

Jack, Florence B., *Cookery for Every Household*. T.C. & E.C. Jack, 1914.

Jack, Florence B. and Strauss, Rita, *The Woman's Book*. T.C. & E.C. Jack, Edinburgh, 1911.

Kirk, Mrs E.W., *Tried Favourites*. Fairgrieve, Edinburgh (21e).

Lees-Dods, Matilda, *The Ideal Home: How to Find it, How to Furnish it, How to Keep it*. Waverley Book Company.

Malcolmson, Patricia, *English Laundresses: a Social History 1850-1930*. University of Illinois Press, 1986.

M'Gonigle, G.C.M. and Kirby, J., *Poverty and Public Health*. Left Book Club, 1936.

Mappen, Ellen, *Helping Women at Work: The Women's Industrial Council 1889-1914* (Explorations in Feminism series). Hutchinson / Explorations in Feminism Collective, 1985.

Marshall, A.C. (ed.), *Complete Illustrated Household Encyclopaedia*, Newnes.

Marshall, A.C. (ed.), *News Chronicle Housewife's Handy Book*. Newnes.

Meighn, Moira, *Simplified Cooking and Invalid Diet*. Faber & Gwyer (The Scienific Press), 1928.

Mercier, Mrs Jerome (ed.), *Work, and How to Do It*. Hatchards, 1885.

Miles, Alfred H. (ed.), *Household Oracle*. Hutchinson & Co.

Minter, Davide C. (ed.), *Book of the Home*. Gresham Publishing Co., 1927.

Morris, T., *Cash Price List*. Stratford-on-Avon.

Newsholme, Arthur and Scott, Margaret Eleanor, *Domestic Economy*. Swan Sonnenschein & Co., 1895.

Peel, Mrs C.S. (ed.), *Daily Mail Cookery Book*. Associated Newspapers, 1920.

Peel, Mrs C.S., *How to Keep House*. Constable, 1906

Peel, Mrs C.S., *How We Lived Then*. John Lane / Bodley Head, 1929.

Percival, Jacqueline, *Breadcrumbs and Banana Skins: the Birth of Thrift*. History Press, 2010.

Pugh, W.T. Gordon, *Practical Nursing, including Hygiene and Dietetics*. William Blackwood, 1936.

Rankin, Margaret Cuthbert, *Art and Practice of Laundry Work*. Blackie & Son.

Reeves, Maud Pember, *Round About a Pound a Week*. Virago, 1979 (first published 1913).

Rice, Margery Spring, *Working-class Wives, their Health and Conditions*. Virago, 1981 (first published 1939).

Rundell, Mrs, *New System of Domestic Cookery*. Milner & Sowerby, Halifax, 1864.

Savings and Savoury Dishes. A. & C. Black, 1917 (5e).

Secrets of Health & Comfort. Lever Brothers Ltd, Port Sunlight.

Seymour, John, *Complete Book of Self Sufficiency*. Faber, 1976.

Silvester, Elizabeth, *Silvester's Sensible Cookery*. Herbert Jenkins (revised and enlarged edn).

Sims, George R. (ed.), *Edwardian London*, Village Press, 1990 (originally published as Living London, 1902).

Simpson, Helen, *Happy Housewife*. Hodder & Stoughton, 1934.

Stacpoole, Florence, *Handbook of Housekeeping for Small Incomes*. Walter Scott Ltd.

Steel, F.A. and Gardiner, G., *Complete Indian Housekeeper and Cook*. Edinburgh Press, Edinburgh, 1893 (3e).

Universal Home Doctor. Odhams.

Vince, Mrs M., *Decoration and Care of the Home*. Collins, 1923.

Wetenhall, Louise, *Practical Laundry Work for Home and School*. Isaac Pitman.

Wigginton, Eliot (ed.), *Foxfire Book* (vol. 1). Anchor Books, New York, 1972.

Wilson, R.J. (ed.), *The Co-operative Managers' Text Book*. Co-operative Union, Manchester, 1915 (re).

Wood, Catherine J., *Handbook of Nursing for the Home and the Hospital*. Cassell & Co., 1897.

Wright, Lawrence, *Clean and Decent: the Fascinating History of the Bathroom and the Water-Closet*. Penguin, 2000 (first published 1960).

You & I Cookery Book, Birling Publishing Co., Birling, Kent.

MAGAZINES

Good Needlework and Knitting Magazine, July 1938 (UK).

Needlecraft: the Magazine of Home Arts, June 1931 (USA).

NEWSPAPERS

Daily Mail, 3 February 1954.

WEBSITES

www.chem-tox.com

www.engineering-timelines.com

http://hansard.millbanksystems.com/lords/1919/nov/rats-and-mice-destruction-bill

INDEX

Abell, Mrs 74
Acme wringers 85
Acts of Parliament 106, 110, 128
Adulterants 87
Airing the washing 86
Alternative remedies 134
Aluminium 11; see Pots and Pans
Ammonia 11, 15, 24, 32, 37, 69, 70, 101
Amputation 136
Anaphylactic shock 134
Ants 121, 122, 125, 127, 129
Appalachian mountain women, method of making soap 75
Appliances, domestic 16
Artificial oil of sassafras 132
Army & Navy Stores 129
Ashes 74-75
Australia 15
Bait 131
Bananas 130
Bath brick / brick dust 11, 22, 24, 92, 95, 96
Bed linen 65, 84
Bed bugs 121, 122, 125, 129
Beds and bedding 130
Beer 130
Beeswax 37, 39, 69, 92
Beetle (for washing) 69
Beetles 125; see Cockroaches
Beeton, Mrs 52, 55
Bicarbonate of soda 132
Black, Clementina 58, 99,
Black American Ashes 74
Black-lead 11, 13, 38
Bleaching 69, 78, 101
Blood poisoning 13
Blue 69, 102
Boiler 65, 66; see Gas
Book of Hints and Wrinkles 18, 29, 37, 86
Book of the Home vol 3 (Humphry) 54, 80, 84, 95, 111

Book of the Home vol 2 (Minter) 30, 38, 77
Borax 37, 88, 131
Bottom drawer 104
Bowls 65
Brandy 135
Brasso 10, 48
Bread 38
Brighton, Sussex 108
Brooke's Soap (Monkey Brand) 12, 18, 22, 24, 53, 70
Broom cupboard 30
Brooms and brushes 15, 38
Brown, Mike and Harris, Carol 95
Brunswick Black 38
'Bulldog spirit' 59
Butter of antimony 14
Calomel 133
Calamine lotion 134
Camp Coffee 103
Camphor 39, 125
Cancer 130
Candles 88, 92
Carbolic acid 133, 134
Carbosil 76
Cardinal polish 17, 26, 40
Carlyle, Jane 121
Carpet 15, 16, 17-18, 38, 39, 41, 127
Carpet sweeper 16
Carson, Rachel: *Silent Spring* 122
Castor oil 130, 133
Caustic soda 74
Cayenne pepper 130
Chemicals 108, 109
Children: and character building 114, 115; head lice 132; and housework 21, 48
Chimney sweep, preparation for visit 37
Chloroform 132
Chloride of lime 36, 68
Chump: see Dolly peg

Cleaning products 10-11, 13, 14-15; see Raw materials; Recipes
Cleanliness and godliness 107, 109
Clothes 16, 17, 63, 66, 85; caps 101; gaiters 99; order of washing 65; poverty and 83; see Body lice; How to clean; Ironing; Irons; Laundry; Linen cupboard; Shirts; Underwear; Washing, etc
Clothes horse 67, 82, 85-86
Clothes line 67
Clothes pegs 67
Clothes sprinkler 77
Coal fires 36, 38
Coal range 11, 20
Cockroaches 121, 125, 129, 130; see Beetles
Common asphaltum 15
Complete Illustrated Household Encyclopaedia (Marshall) 16, 31, 81
Concise Household Encyclopedia (Hammerton) 96, 136
Cookery for Every Household (Jack) 32
Co-op 111-112
Co-operative housekeeping 58
'Copper'; see Boiler
Copper stick 66
Corrosive sublimate 129, 130
Corsets, cleaning 96-97
Craig, Elizabeth 34
Crickets 121, 125
Cross infection 132
Cucumber 130
Culpeper, Nicholas 70, 133
Cyanide of potassium 131-132
DDT 122-5, 136
Daily Mail Cookery Book (Peel, Mrs C.S.) 59
Davidson, Caroline 63
Demon beetle trap 125
Detergents 101

Dickens, Charles 85
Dictionary of Daily Wants 122, 135
Disease prevention 73
Disinfectant 26, 35, 126
Dodd, Marguerite (*America's Homemaking Book*) 122; see DDT
Dog bites 134-135
Dolly peg 68, 76, 77
Dolly tub 68, 77
Donkeystone; see Hearthstone
Doors 21, 28
Drake, Barbara 110
Dripping 74
Dry Soon 87
Dry cleaning 97, 113
Drying the washing 63, 82, 83, 87, 106; see Lakeland
Dust 10, 15, 35
Dust destructor 35
Dustbin 32, 34-35, 36
Dusters 65
Dustpan and brush 15
Earwigs 121
Eco-Dry 87
Ediswan vacuum cleaners 25
Eggshells 22
Electric appliances 30, 81, 82; see also Irons; Washing machines
Electric shock 63, 83
Electrical Association for Women 95
Electricity 13, 16, 17, 20, 25, 96, 126; see also Homes
Employment 46, 52; see also Servants
Enemas 133; see Soap
Enquire Within upon Everything (1910) 122
Enquire Within upon Everything (1940s) 122
Era Moth Killer Cartridge and Wardrobe Sachet 129
Eradico 129
Fabric 76, 77-78, 83, 84, 88, 96, 97, 99, 100-102
Family 33, 41; see also Children; Spring Cleaning
Fareham, Hampshire 129

Feather boas, cleaning 97
Feather curlers; see Sweated labour
Fireplace 33
First aid 133-134
Five Step Method; see School
Flannels 65, 88, 89; cleaning 100-101; Jaeger brand 100-101; see Underwear
Flatleys 87
Fleas 121, 122, 130, 132, 135; see DDT
Flies 121, 122, 125, 127, 130-131; see DDT
'Floor duster' 17
Floor polisher 17; see Electricity
Floors: cleaning 15-16; dusting 15, 17; linoleum 18, 19; stone 18; sweeping carpet 15; tiled 18, 40; wooden 17-18, 27, 43, 44; see also Indian matting; Recipes
Flour 23
Fly papers 130, 132; see Tanglefoot
Flypic 129
Food, decanting 32
Formalin 129
Fumigation 129
Gaiters, cleaning 99
Garden soil 133
Gas 13, 20, 30, 95, 100; cleaning a gas stove 41; drying cabinets 86; irons 94, 95; washing boilers 66; washing machines 82; mangles and wringers 85; see Homes; Irons
Gilbreth, Lillian 31
Girls, training for future 114-115
Girls Friendly Society 46; see Mercier, Mrs Jerome; Servants
Glue 19-20
Glycerine 102
Gnat bites 133
Goffering tongs 68
Gonorrhoea 70
Government policy and servants 57-58, 59
Grass 15
Grease, removing 68, 69, 72, 101; see Soap

Great Ormond Street Hospital: see Wood, Catherine
Great War 57, 80, 90, 99, 104, 133; see Servants
Grebe skin, cleaning 97
Green, W.H. 128
Green tea 130
Greenwich linoleum 18
Gum arabic 68, 88, 102
Gum water 99, 101, 103
Hair brushes, cleaning 97
Harpic 11
Hartshorn 24
Haslett, Caroline 95
Hay 103
Hearthstone 10-11
Hero mouse trap 131
Hog's lard 126
Home Book (Mrs D.D. Cottington Taylor) 19, 21, 56
Home of To-day 77
Homes: clean 121; cupboard space 104; dirty 121; lacking facilities 13, 115; middle class 10-11, 16; 19th century 9, 121; and pests 121; and sanitation 121; slums 14; small 28; 20th century 126; upper class 103; working class 106; see Electricity; Gas; Interior decoration; London; Pests
Honey 132
Hopper 75; see Soap, making
House design examined 31
House furnishings 121, 127
Housewives 9, 11, 13, 14-15, 26; excessively house-proud 32; forlorn advice to 129; long hours 32; and pests 121-122; skills 87, 115, 117; unpaid 34; see Family; Housework; Mother-daughter relationship; Servants
Housework 9, easier 126; and madness 32; over-zealous 126; primitive tools 59; standards 32, 39; timetables 34; see Floors; Housewives; Laundry work; Spring cleaning; Step cleaning

INDEX

PAGE 145

Hygiene and sanitation 73, 101, 121
Income 13-14, 28, 78, 80; and budget overhaul 42; reducing expenses 54; see Vince, Mrs
India 134
Indian matting 18
Infectious diseases 108, 109
Interior decoration 17, 66; summer and winter 36
Iodine 132
Ipecacuanha 134
Iron 135
Ironing 101-102, board 67; cleaning 92, 94, 95; polishing board 67; shirt board 67; sleeve board 67; table 67; see Lace; Underwear
Irons 90, 94, 95; box 68, 90, 91; calender machines 91; charcoal 68; egg 93; electric 25, 30, 90, 95; flat 67, 90, 91, 92; gas 91, 94, 95, 111; goffering 91, 93, 94; Italian / Dalli / tally 68, 91, 92, 93-94; pagoda stoves 94; polishing 68, 91, 94; 'sad' 92; shields 94; slippers 94, 96; temperature 91, 92, 94, 95; see Electric; Gas; Prices
Isinglass 88
Jack, Florence 24, 32, 47, 99, 103, 113
Jackson's 17
Jewellers' rouge 15
Kitchen cabinets 29, 30, 31, 127
Kitchens 127: blue 130; new ideas and 59; and servants 43; small gadgets 31; streamlined 32; see Kitchen cabinets; Pots and pans; Servants; Spring cleaning; Washing up etc
Knives 10-11, 21-22, 23-24; see also Lansard; Servants
Labour saving 28-32, 43, 58, 80, 94, 96, 126
Lace 65; cleaning 101-103; lace punch 68, 103
Lakeland 77, 87
Lamp oil, removing 27
Lansard Knife Cleaning and Sharpening Machine 10
Larders 128
Launderettes 106, 113
Laundries, small 113
Laundries, commercial 63, 91, 96, 102, 108, 109-114; see also Acts of Parliament; Co-op; Drake, Barbara; Gas, London; MacDonald, Margaret; Prices
Laundry, home 98
Laundry workers 83, 88
Leather 23, 24, 38
Lee, Lord Arthur 129
Lees-Dods, Matilda 98, 105
Lemon husks 23
Lever Brothers 73
Lice, body 133; head 132; see also DDT; Parasites
Lidded bucket for washing day 77
Lifebuoy soap 11, 70
Lime 74; unslacked 27
Linen, storage and care 103, 104, 109; assigned to servants 104; list for upper-class homes 104; see Laundries; Prices; Tablecloths
Linseed oil 14, 15, 39
Lions 75
Lockjaw 133
London 14, 35, 51, 106, 107, 114
Lux 70, 72
Lye 69, 75
MacDonald, Margaret / Women's Industrial Council 113
Magazines 72, 104
Mangles and mangling 63, 66, 67, 83, 84, 85-86, 106; see Wringers
Manufacturers, exaggerated claims made by 73, 82
Mansion Polish 17, 19
Marble, cleaning 39, 42
Marriage 54, 104; and servants 46
Massage 39; see Shampooing
Meighn, Moira on cancer 130
Mercier, Mrs Jerome 46-47
Mercury 70, 133

Mesh screens 130
Methylated spirit 15, 37, 38, 68, 91, 95
Mice: see Rats and mice
Middle class women as laundry managers 113-4; training up servants 46
Milk 18, 103, 131, 134
Min Cream 21
Monel 30
Mop 17
Morality 111, 115
Morrison, W S 128
Mosquitoes 121, 122; bites 132; see DDT
Moths 36, 121, 127
Mother-daughter relationship 9-10, 64, 115
Multi-use appliances and furniture 80, 86
Muslin 65, 84, 88, 101, 131
Mustard plaster 135
National Grid 95
Needlecraft magazine (USA) 71, 72
Nelson Brothers (Nelson, Dale & Co) 51
Nettles 131
New Zealand meat: see Nelson Bothers; Servants
Newsholme, Arthur 107-108
Newsholme, Arthur and Scott, Margaret Eleanor 68, 79, 107, 108
Newspaper 15, 36
Nit nurse 132
Nixey's black-lead 11
North America 15, 31, 72, 74, 75
Nursing textbooks, 19th century 133
O-Cedar 17; Fly Spray 129
Oatmeal 76
Oil of lavender 125
Oil of male fern 133
Oil of turpentine 22, 129
Oil paintings, cleaning 39
Oleic acid 39
Onions 133-134
Online search 130

Oxalic acid 63, 69
P & G 72
Paraffin 23, 38, 39, 63, 129, 132
Parasites: body lice 132; head lice 132; scabies 133; tapeworms 133; threadworms 133; see also Lice
Pearlashes 27
Pear's soap 70
Peel, Mrs C.S. 55, 59; see Kitchens; Tweeny
Peppermint essence 132
Perfume 76
Permanganate of potash 69
Persian powder 130
Pests 115, 121, 122, 124, 126, 129
Petrol 63, 68, 97
Phosphorus 122, 126
Phossy jaw 122
Pioneer Chain Driven Mangle 80
Pipemaker's clay 14
Plate powder 24
Poisons / toxics 68, 83; see Calomel; Mercury; Oxalic acid; Phosphorus; Quicksilver; Salts of lemon; Salts of sorrel
Polish: floor 10, 17; furniture 10, 11, 39; metal 10, 39, 48; Min 21; see Raw materials; Recipes
Portsmouth, Hampshire 11, 129
Posser 76: see Dolly peg
Potash 74
Potatoes 23, 39, 87, 90, 99
Pots and pans 20, 70; aluminium 22; brass and copper 22, 48; enamel ware 22; enamelled ironware 22; iron 22; japanned 23; non-stick 22; pewter 23
Pounding 69, 78
Poverty 13, 70, 114
Powdered chalk 39; see Powdered whiting
Powdered parsley seed 132
Powdered resin 130
Powdered whiting 15, 22, 23, 24, 39; see Powdered chalk

Prices: 13, 14, 19, 21, 25, 26, 33, 40, 48, 65, 67-68 70, 78, 80, 82, 86, 94, 95, 99, 103-104, 106, 110, 113; see Washing equipment, prices
Prop 67
Pulley 67, 82
Punch 76: see Dolly peg
Pyrethrum 130, 131, 133
Quassia 125
Quicklime 129
Quicksilver 24
Rankin, Margaret Cuthbert (*Art and Practice of Laundry Work*) 65, 66, 67, 77, 83, 84, 86, 93, 94, 116
Rats and mice 121, 126, 128, 129, 130, 131, 136
Raw materials 14-15
Recipes 17, 36, 39, 73, 76
Reckitt & Colman 11, 17: see also Reckitt & Sons, and products
Reckitt & Sons 26; see also Reckitt & Colman, and products
Recycling 75
Refuse, household 35-36, 66
Registry Office 47; see Servants
Remedies: old fashioned 133; 19th century 125-126; 20th century 126
Rice 87
Rinso 70, 71
River 63, 69
Robin Starch 87
Ronuk 17
Rottenstone 14, 22
Sal volatile 132
Salt 22, 68, 123, 130
Salts of lemon 68
Salts of sorrel 68
San-pic disinfectant 26, 126
Sand / silver sand 20, 22-23, 27, 39
Sanitas 18
Santonin 133; see Urine
Sapolio 18, 22, 24, 70
School 63, 64: Domestic Science 114; Five Step Method 116; laundrywork 115-117; teenagers 117
Scorpion stings 134-135
Scrubbing mix 39
Servantless houses 28-29, 34
Servants: advice to 27, 46; allowances 51-52; alternative employment 45; and precious ornaments 42, 46; beer 52; butler 56; decline in numbers of 43; demeaning work 46; and drink 47; enticements 59; extravagance 54; followers 52-53; food 50-51; government policy and 57-58, 59; and Great War 28, 45, 57; hard work 28, 38, 47, 55; health and welfare 27, 43; housework 18, 20, 24, 43, 45; hygiene 20; and knives 10; and labour saving 43; personality clashes 54, 55, 57; at pivotal point of domestic history 45; religion 47; selling perquisites 54; the servant problem 43, 47; slapdash habits 24; as status symbols 43; time off 47, 50; timetables 49; training of 43, 46; uppity nature of 47; see Girls Friendly Society; Jack, Florence; Lees-Dods, Matilda; Peel, Mrs C.S.; Registry Office; Servantless household; Stacpoole, Florence; Thompson, Flora; Tweeny
Servants' duties: cook 49; 'cook-general' 45; house parlourmaid 47, 49-50
Seymour, John (*Complete Book of Self-Sufficiency*) 75
Shampooing: see Massage
Shirts 65, 90
Shops 10, 11; see Army & Navy
Silk, cleaning 97
Silver nitrate 134
Silverfish 131-132, 136
Silvester, Elizabeth: on labour saving 58;
Silvo 10, 56
Sims, George R. (*Edwardian London*) 107

Sinks 24, 30
Small beer 14
Snake bites 134-135
Snuff 125, 130
Soap 13, 14, 18, 23, 24, 70, 97; bulk buying 70; medicinal uses 70, 73; used as shampoo 72; see also Enemas
Soap, bars 70
Soap, carbolic 37, 70, 76
Soap, carpet 41
Soap flakes 11, 70
Soap, gritty 12
Soap, making 63, 72, 74, 75, 76
Soap, soft 14, 15, 22, 37, 39
Soap jelly 70, 73, 100
Soap tax 69
Soapmakers' Company 74
Soapwort 69
Social networking 9, 107
Social surveys 13
Soda 11, 13, 22 , 23, 24, 36, 37, 39, 42, 68, 97, 99; and skin 13, 38; see Blood poisoning
Sodium fluoride 131
South America 70
Spirits of naphtha 129
Spirits of salt 14
Spirits of wine 14, 24, 39
Sponges, cleaning 98
Spring cleaning 9, 37, 38, 39, 41, 42, 60; bedroom 37-38; exhaustion 41; hilarity of 36; kitchen and scullery 41-42; less need for 39; see Cleaning products; Family, Recipes
Stacpoole, Florence (Handbook of housekeeping for small incomes) 50, 51
Stains 67-68, 72
Starch and starching 63, 69, 87-88, 90, 99, 101, 102
Stavesacre ointment 133
Steam: disinfecting with 132
Steel, F.A. and Gardiner, G. (*Complete Indian Housekeeper and Cook*) 134-135

Step cleaning 9
Stings 133
Stone blue 14
Stone potash 15
Suction washer 77
Sugar 88, 102, 125
Sulphur 130, 132; see Parasites; Pests
Sunlight soap 11, 70
Sunshades and parasols, cleaning 99; see Prices; Sweated labour
Swans down, cleaning 100
Sweated labour 97, 99-100
Sweeping 15
Sweet oil 23, 32
Table linen 65, 68, 104-105; folding large tablecloths 105
Tanglefoot mixture 130
Tar 131
Tea dyeing 102
Tea leaves 102-103; cleaning floors 15, 17; see Servants
Thrift 73, 76, 98, 99
Time and motion 31
Trampling 69, 77
Tried Favourites (Kirk) 74
Turpentine 15, 17, 39, 68, 88
Tweeny 55, 59; see Peel, Mrs C.S.; Servants
Underwear: see Flannels
Ure, Doctor 126
Urine 133; washing clothes in 63, 69
Vacuum cleaner 17, 25; and DDT 122; see Electricity
Verdigris 22
Veto mouse trap 131
Vince, Mrs 42-43
Vinegar 14, 22, 39, 68, 132-133
Waring & Gillow 103
Warts and verrucas 134
Washboard 66, 76, 83
Washhouse 63, 106-107; see Prices; Social networking
Washing: correct order of doing 65; hard work 63, 67, 76, 82, 83; lack of facilities at home 116; only satisfaction of 117; traditional

methods 63, 77
Washing day hazards 63, 69, 77, 78, 80, 83, 84, 96, 97
Washing equipment: small items 68; prices 65, 67-68, 70, 78, 80, 82, 86, 94, 95
Washing machines 76, 77, 81, 82; affordable 113; Bradford Vowel Washing Machine 67, 80, 84; Bradford Vowel Ito 80; Dolly model 80, 84; HMV washing machine 81; manual filling and emptying 82; Summerscales Household Washer 78, 79; see Electricity; Gas
Washing tubs 65, 77
Washing up 11, 20, 23-24, 29, 73; washing up liquid 20, 23
Wasps 121; stings 133
Water 10, 13, 14, 78, 106; hard 72; lack of 63, 75, 116; softening 68, 69, 72; soapy 102; soft 72
Wetenhall, Louise (*Practical Laundry Work*) 91, 93, 111
Wheelie bins 35, 36
Whisky 126
White arsenic 130
White wax 69
Wimbledon Laundry Company 114
Windolene 11
Windows, cleaning 11
Wintergreen 129
Witch hazel 134
Wood: draining boards 27, 32; scrubbing 24, 27
Wood, Catherine 73
Woodworm 127
Working classes, health of 82, 106
Wormwood 129
Wringers: Bradford Acorn Wringer 85; Bradford Premier Box Mangle 86; see Mangles
Wright, Lawrence 73
Zebo grate cleaner 126, 133

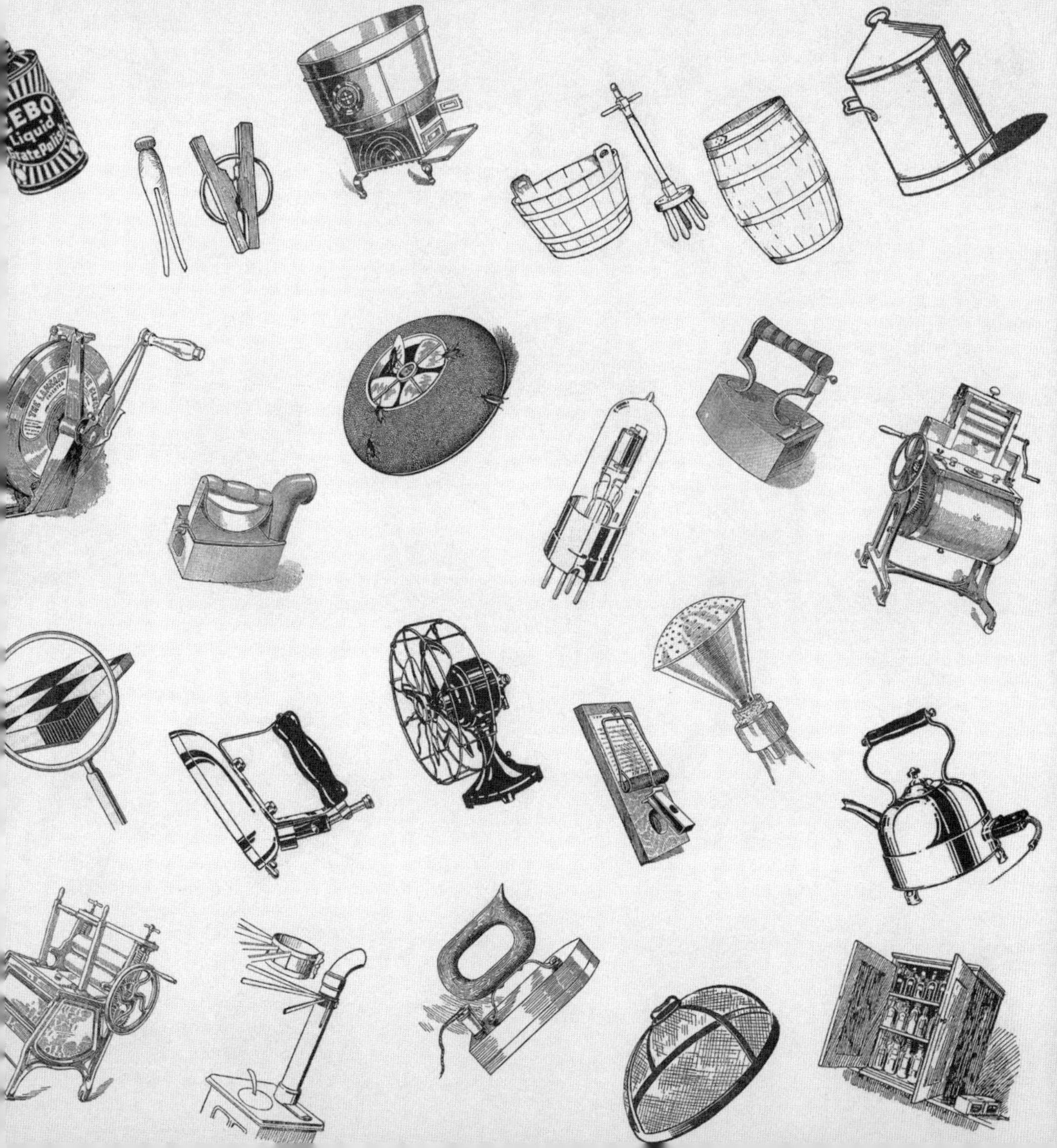
EBO
Liquid

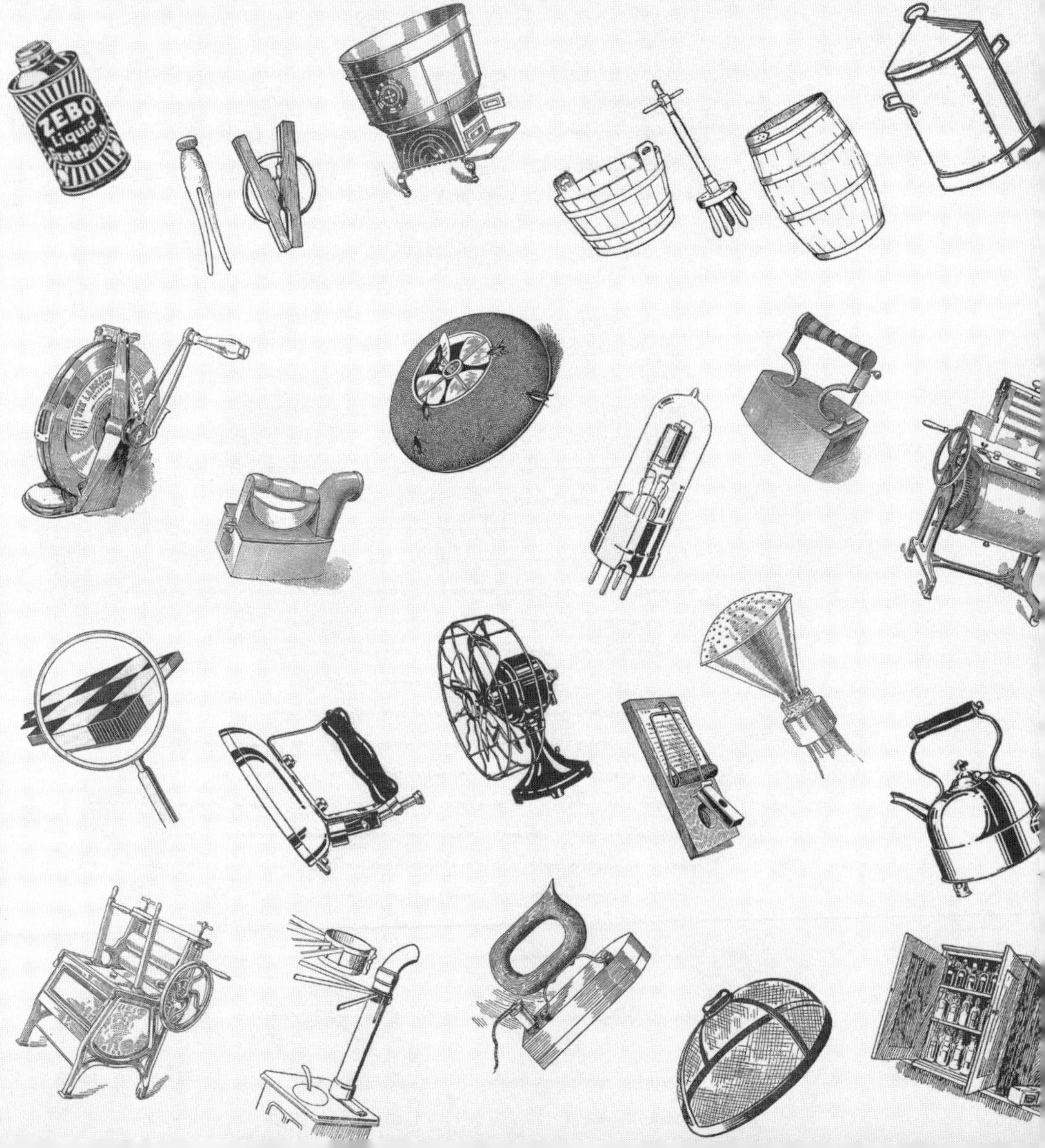
ZEBO
Liquid
Grate Polish